SPARK:

WOMEN IN THE BUSINESS OF CHANGING THE WORLD

Red Thread Publishing LLC. 2022

Write to info@redthreadbooks.com if you are interested in publishing with Red Thread Publishing. Learn more about publications or foreign rights acquisitions of our catalog of books: www.redthreadbooks.com

Copyright © 2022

All rights reserved.

No part of this book may be reproduced in any form or means. Any unauthorized use, sharing, reproduction or distribution of these materials by any means, electronic, mechanical or otherwise is strictly prohibited. No portion of these materials may be reproduced in any manner whatsoever, without the express written consent of the publisher, except for the use of brief quotations in a book review.

Paperback ISBN: 9781955683203

Ebook ISBN: 978195568328

Cover Design: Sierra Melcher

Cover Photo by @cullansmithon Unsplash.

CONTENTS

Dedication   v
Introduction   vii

Let your Spark be Contagious	1
Sierra Melcher	11
The Moments That Define Us	12
Jenny Watz	21
Sparking Genius	22
Adrienne MacIain, PhD	31
Permission for Pleasure	32
Elizabeth Cartagena	41
Unleashing Women in Leadership	42
Dr. Hynd Bouhia	51
Adversity - Your Greatest Gift	52
Reem Borrows	65
Making Lemonade from Lemons	66
Josephine S N Kalagira	75
The Trek to Helping Others and Changing the World	76
Rena McDonald	85
Redefining Customer Service	86
Judy Granlee-Gates	95
A Marketing Love Story: Ideas to change the game	97
Dannie Cadavid	105
Grit	106
Poet Khan Rass Fiyaa	115
Breaking the Pattern of Emotional Addiction	117
Destiny DeHaven	125
Red Thread Publishing	127
THANK YOU!	129
CALL FOR SUBMISSIONS	131
Acknowledgements	133

ALSO BY RED THREAD BOOKS	135
FEISTY: Dangerously Amazing Women Using Their Voices & Making An Impact	137
SANCTUARY: Cultivating Safe Space, Rediscovering the Power that United Us	139
Notes	141

DEDICATION

May the future be different than the past.

INTRODUCTION
BY ADRIENNE MACIAIN, PHD

Women have always been leaders. Anyone who thinks otherwise has clearly never birthed and raised a human being from scratch.

Yet women's leadership has, for far too long, been relegated to the domestic realm, the spark within us to embrace our full power, empower our communities, and improve our world deliberately snuffed out at every turn.

The spark, however, burns on, and has only gotten hotter and brighter through the years.

The stories in this book are true tales of life lessons learned by women who have answered the call to leadership, and embraced the challenge of allowing their spark to burn brightly, in business and beyond, despite the very real risks of standing out and speaking up.

May their wisdom inspire you to fan the flames of your own authority, and to show up and shine as the natural born leader (a.k.a. BOSS BABE) you are and have always been.

Your spark is needed. Your stories and your wisdom are needed. Your courageous leadership is needed.

Blaze on!

LET YOUR SPARK BE CONTAGIOUS
BY SIERRA MELCHER

"Our deepest fear is not that we are inadequate. Our deepest fear is that we are powerful beyond measure. ... Your playing small does not serve the world. ... We are all meant to shine, as children do. ...And as we let our own light shine, we unconsciously give other people permission to do the same. As we are liberated from our own fear, our presence automatically liberates others."
— Marianne Williamson, A Return to Love: Reflections on the Principles of "A Course in Miracles"

I believe in a world where the stories in our hearts are the books that will change the world, but only if we write them!

THE BOOK TRAPPED in your heart, locked in your mind won't change diddly-shit. I know this all too well. For so long, I believed I needed to first change the world before I could write a book. I needed to fix myself, get my shit together, be all that, *so that* I could write a book. I believed that I needed to become the authority before I could have permission to write a book.

A few years ago, I dared to do it anyway. I wrote and published my first book. What I learned, and now fundamentally understand, is that by doing the work of writing my story, I earned the right. I became the expert, the credible source, the authority.

BY WRITING THE BOOK, I was transformed. By publishing the book, I changed the world.

Writing a book requires three things:

1. Courage
2. Structure: the container, the guide, the outline, the map
3. Opportunity

Despite what you may think, only one of these three is your responsibility, or even within your control.

As with so many things, believing we have to do it all ourselves puts undue pressure and responsibility on us. When we expect too much of ourselves, often we quit before we can even try. So remember: only 1/3 of this is on you. It's an important third; no one can do it for you. The courage, the willingness to tell your story, to share your experience and your wisdom, to show up vulnerably, authentically, and imperfectly, just as you are. That is no small feat.

BUT HONEY, *the rest is not on you!*

Red Thread offers the other 2/3rds: the structure, and the opportunity, if you're willing to seize it. We've built a clear, simple map from your draft to publication, and beyond. We've tried it a bunch of ways, made a bunch of mistakes. We know a lot of pathways you should *not* go down, and we know others that will genuinely support you, where you can thrive. We've built the structure for you so that all you have to do is show up with your courage and follow the map.

The opportunity is not on you, either. You don't have to start a publishing company, and you don't need to become an expert at everything that goes into a successful book launch. You just have to tell your story, the part that no one else can do for you.

RED THREAD PROVIDES the opportunity for your book to make a real impact. We've built the structure, and the container, and we're constantly improving both. We create the opportunity every day so that all you have to do is show up with your story, your vision, your message, and the courage to share it.

We are unique in the publishing world, in that in addition to publishing, we offer support, guidance, and education through every phase of the process: ideation, writing & revision, publication, and most importantly, building a purpose and passion-based business using authority marketing and expert positioning, so that each of our authors optimizes the visibility and credibility cultivated by publishing her book.

Red Thread Publishing is an all-female, nonfiction publishing company. We are on a mission to support 10,000 women to become not only successful published authors, but thought leaders, thereby changing both their lives and the world. When 10,000 women write and publish their books, they transform themselves into authorities in their field, and become thought leaders.

Hold the phone, drop the mic. *Holy fucking shit!* Just bask for a moment in the epic impact of women not just changing but *leading* the conversation, on a global scale. When we change the conversation, we change ourselves & we change the trajectory of history.

Make no mistake: *we are changing the world.*

I FOUNDED a publishing company so that I could take all that I had learned in my own process and multiply that impact exponentially. If I'd had such support available to me when I started dreaming of writing, 15+ years ago, who knows what I could have accomplished by now? I wanted other women writers to have a better experience, and a greater impact, than any one of us could have on our own. Little did I know what building this business would lead me to discover...

This is my Ikigai. You know, that Japanese concept that means, essentially, the sweet spot of your gifts: the value you bring, mission, purpose, and talent? The diagram below shows a series of intersecting circles: what you do for money, what you're great at, what you love, and what the world needs. The little space in the very center where all four of these elements intersect is Ikigai.

Through Red Thread Publishing, I absolutely have discovered my Ikigai, and I want the same for you, and for every woman. Let what lights you up be contagious. Let your passion transform your life and ripple out to spark passion in others.

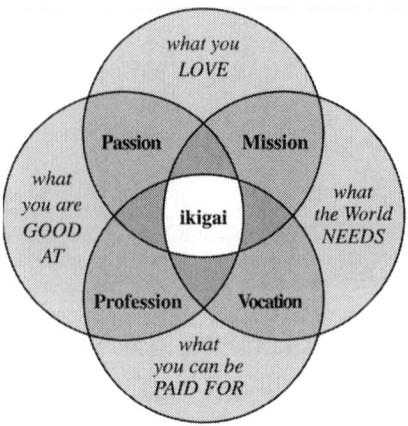

TRUE STORIES...

One author thought her career was over. She'd had a negative experience with the publishing industry, but decided to take a chance on publishing two books with us last year. Instantly, she was reinvigorated, and praised by so many of her fans. Since then, she has *lit it up* every damn day, and even founded a new international network for women. She told us, "Publishing my books with you literally saved my life."

Another woman joined us after self-publishing a few books on her own. Frustrated with the lack of traction her existing books were getting despite all the work she'd gone through and all the money she'd spent on them, she was ready to throw in the towel. Then she discovered Red Thread, where she found the community, the support, and the guidance she needed to make the publishing process as easy and enjoyable as she had always wanted to believe it could be. Not only is she now the proud book mom of a brand new bestselling release, thanks to the Red Thread "Beyond the Book" guidance and support, she was able to create a course to go with it, build a business around her own Ikigai, and even make major headway on her next book!

As she put it: "I've navigated this process alone, and I've sailed through it in the delightful company of a supportive community of incredible women. Needless to say, I am never, ever, EVER going back."

A FIRST-TIME AUTHOR who wrote a chapter in one of our books was overcome with emotion the moment she held the book in her hands. When she saw her own chapter, with her own name, her own words, and even her own image and author bio, she immediately began to cry. It's a powerful moment. It's impossible not to see ourselves differently when we see it there in black and white. That's me. I am an author. I wrote that. I've shared my gifts with the world.

That's the gift we want to offer to 10,000 women. Will you be one of them?

TAKE a look at the list of books we've helped bring forth this year, as well as the authors that have already joined our community & will be published soon. Can you imagine your book on that list? https://redthreadbooks.mykajabi.com/books

. . .

ONE OF THE transformations that I love to witness with our authors and clients is this: the women who come to publish with us or even just to learn from us come with more or less the same questions:
- What if I can't?
- What if nobody cares what I have to say?
- What if I don't have anything of value to add?
- What if I'm not a writer?

These doubts and fears are so common. Sometimes they're voiced directly. Sometimes they're subtle hints. In my experience, these questions are universal, and often paralyzing. Whether we ever admit them to ourselves, or come out with these doubts and fears blazing, we think we are keeping ourselves safe by not trying.

WHAT HAPPENS, though, when we walk a woman through this writing process, and this publishing process, is that she finds a new way to tell her story. She begins to relate to herself differently. I recently heard a woman in our author community reporting exactly this:

"I finished my first draft. I feel really good about it. I didn't know I had it in me. When I read my own work, I'm stunned. It's not yet done. It's not perfect. But it really is amazing. And I'm beginning to see myself differently. I'm beginning to see myself as I've always wanted to, as a writer, and I'm seeing a new destination."

This woman is still in the beginning of this process. But she's already having an epic transformation. This is incredible. This is why the work we do is so important to me. Why it fills me up, lights me up, gets me up early in the morning to do it again. It fuels me when things get hard. Because things DO get hard.

EVERY SINGLE TIME a woman holds her book in her hands for the first time, something fundamental clicks and changes in her. Maybe she sees a new woman in the mirror after seeing that face on the back of a book. Maybe, like me, a few months go by, and she picks up her book, turns to a page, reads a little bit and thinks, "Wow. That's great. I wish somebody had told me that earlier!" Hardly even realizing that *those are her own words*.

That book is her gift to the world, and to every woman who needs the wisdom she has gained through experience, herself very much included.

THE NEW QUESTION

What happens when we become authors? When we hold our book babies, when we go through this journey, this transformation, we have a new question.

IT'S NO LONGER: *What if I can't? What if no one cares? What if no one likes it? What if I'm not good enough?*

The new question becomes: *What else can I do?*

I WANT you to breathe with that one. Because, for me, all of my work can be summarized in that one question. If the only gift I could give anyone or everyone forever forward, it would be that shift out of self-limitation and into limitless possibility.

For me, it's in that space of possibility and confidence and striving that we find our Ikigai. What else can I do that lights me up? What else can I do to earn money? What else can I do that the world needs?

What else can I bring that is uniquely mine? How can I share my gifts with more and more women as they begin to ask themselves these questions?

THE WORLD IS CHANGING. Certainly, but not only for these women individually, and not just for the people they're in contact with. But the epic ripple, the holographic effect of a handful of women coming at life and work and the world differently from this new space to me, it's everything. It is that spark that can catch a wildfire that can truly change the world.

It is more than just writing your book & seeing it in print. We consciously teach our authors how to begin to show up as the authorities & experts they are, well before we go to print. We begin becoming, before there is any visible proof of the change taking place.

We at Red Thread often talk about a book like a baby we are bringing to life. Early in the stages of pregnancy, you may not look pregnant, but there are still plenty of important changes happening. The same is true for our authors.

The book is not the end. It is not even the product. It is just the beginning. A book is a foundation for a woman to launch from to discover her voice, her impact, her power. Her book is her vehicle for her voice & her mission. A book is a way for her to accelerate and amplify her gifts to share with countless others without draining her soul, her spirit, and her bank account. A book is one of the oldest intellectual technological tools. Books are a way for knowledge and information to be stored, transported, and shared. Historically speaking, books changed the world. The printing press changed the world again. We can read the words and ideas of someone who's been dead for centuries.

WITH EACH BOOK on your bookshelf, you're essentially getting to spend hundreds of hours learning with someone in a few 100 pages, you get the combination of a lifetime's experience, wisdom, knowledge, and when that person is gone, that book will last forever. It's an incredible tool, intellectually and spiritually.

For far too long, the vast majority of thinkers who have been celebrated and commemorated in this way have been men. The dominant story that has shaped the world for over 5,000 years has been that of men.

The perceptions, perspectives, and values that have shaped the world, in all cultures have been skewed. We are bringing an alternative to that conversation to bring balance.

WE TEACH our authors how to share their stories in ways that are uniquely theirs. Not by pretending to be someone else or trying to emulate someone they appreciate. But by drilling down into figuring out who they are, because their message is precisely what someone else is needing at this moment. The confidence we gain when we learn how to do that is invaluable. The impact we have is incredible.

It's this kind of development that shows me the power of the magical question: What else can I do? Women come to us thinking that writing a book and publishing is nearly impossible. And when they do it, they begin to wonder: what else have I dismissed as impossible that's been possible all along? What else do I *want* to do?

SHARE **your spark**

"Hide not your talents. They for use were made. What's a sundial in the shade?"
–Benjamin Franklin

When I think about Spark and what it means to be in the business of changing the world, the biggest changes don't happen on the large scale, on the grand stage. Those big changes freak me out, quite honestly. They overwhelm me, and I'm often paralyzed.

The way I show up to change the world is this: one woman at a time, one story at a time.

Because, first of all, that's enough. And second of all, with each of these journeys, with each of these women, it's so much more than just her. That's what the Red Thread logo represents: the ripple effect that is set off by each and every woman who accepts the challenge to share her voice in a world that has worked so diligently to keep her quiet.

. . .

THE RIPPLE BEGINS WITHIN, as she learns to trust her intuition, share her authentic voice, and believe in her own expertise. Then it makes its way out into the world, as her words inspire and impact others, some of whom will see their own story reflected in those words and feel seen, understood, and no longer alone, and they in turn are inspired to share their own unique voices and stories.

And so the ripple begins again. And again. And again.

The writing and publishing process is only the first step in a chain reaction that will continue to impact the author, her community, her readers, and everyone they come into contact with, for a very long time to come.

AS AN ASPIRING AUTHOR, it's so easy to think of the publish date, the book, as the end goal, the finish line. What we know, and remind our authors again and again, is that birthing your book is just the very beginning. The day your book is born is day one. Then comes the life of the book, and of the woman as a published author. That's when we get to play out all those possibilities, the "What else can I do?"

So gather your courage, and begin writing. We will support you with structure and opportunity. Who knows who you will become, and what your spark will set ablaze...

SIERRA MELCHER

Best-selling author, international speaker & educator, Sierra Melcher is founder of *Red Thread Publishing LLC*. She leads an all-female publishing company, with a mission to support 10,000 women to become successful published authors & thought-leaders. Offering world-class coaching & courses that focus on community, collaboration, and a uniquely feminine approach at every stage of the author process.

Sierra has a Master's degree in education, has spoken & taught around the world. Originally from the United States, Sierra lives in Medellin, Colombia with her young daughter.

linktr.ee/redthreadpublishing

THE MOMENTS THAT DEFINE US
BY JENNY WATZ

We all have defining moments in our lives. You know, those times that change us in some way, for better or worse. Maybe there's a song that reminds us of the prom or our first kiss, or we can recount in precise detail when someone asks us where we were on 9/11. These moments trigger memories and help define who we are as human beings. I've had many defining moments that contributed to who I am, but I've also had defining years.

Those defining years began in 2016 when I found myself laid off for the first time in my twenty-plus-year career. After decades of steady employment and upward career mobility, I found myself in the unemployment line. Even though I sort of knew the layoff was coming, I wasn't prepared for the flood of feelings that followed.

Those feelings shocked me.

Mad. Sad. Deflated. Defeated. I felt betrayed, not only by the employer to whom I'd been loyal for more than seven years, but by my entire career and my education. Sure, I tried to put a positive spin on it and give myself a pep talk:

Today is full of opportunity. When one door closes, another one opens. Blah, blah, blah. Bullshit, bullshit, bullshit.

WHO WAS I KIDDING? I couldn't see any opportunity. And as I searched for another job, all I found were more closed doors. Not closed, really. More like bolted shut. I applied for jobs that were a little above my skill level and jobs that I was insanely qualified for. It didn't matter. I didn't have enough experience. I had too much experience. Mad. Sad. Deflated. Defeated.

Depressed.

And for someone who struggles with depression, even on a good day, I didn't need more piled on top. I sunk low, lower than I'd been in a long time. I hadn't realized how much of my self-worth was tied to my job.

But why wouldn't it be? That's how we define ourselves, isn't it? When someone asks us what we do for a living, we respond with "I am" statements. "I'm a writer." "I'm an accountant." "I'm (insert job title here)."

Why do we do that? That's not who we *are*. It's what we *do*. So naturally when I got laid off, I became more depressed because I went from being something to being… nothing. I'm not a writer or an accountant or anything else.

I am nothing.

During that time, I became an expert at binge-watching shows on Netflix. I forced myself to walk the dog every day even though I didn't feel like it. Some days I took a shower. Some days I didn't. My life was devoid of purpose.

Then I was approached by a former colleague of mine about a contract job opportunity. She had just started a job with an agricultural commodity organization and wanted to delegate one of the responsibilities to someone else so she could focus on other core aspects of the position. The opportunity called for someone to serve as managing editor for a trade publication, doing everything from brainstorming content ideas to researching topics, interviewing subject matter experts, and drafting articles, to working with graphic designers on layout and providing editing and proofing of the entire publication prior to printing and distribution. And since my experience included writing and editing along with fifteen years of working with agriculture industry clients, I said yes.

That opportunity represented my first foray into the world of freelancing. With a renewed sense of purpose, I tackled that opportunity and searched for others. You see, by this time I had read enough tea leaves to conclude that no one else was going to hire me on a full-time basis, so it was time I hired myself. Full-time freelancing, here I come!

AT FIRST I focused on finding clients in the food and agriculture industries, because that's what I knew. After all, I'd spent the past fifteen years of my life working with those industries. But the clients didn't come. And I soon realized that I lacked passion for those industries. Maybe because getting laid off took the wind out of my sails, or maybe because that's never really where my heart was.

I started searching for my passion. I asked my friends and family members what they thought I was good at. Some of them thought I was fishing for compliments, but I wasn't. I was honestly trying to figure out what other people perceived my strengths to be. Maybe they saw a strength I didn't see in myself or didn't consider to be a strength. Maybe I could capitalize on some of those strengths to create a sustainable business.

Overwhelmingly, people responded by telling me that I'm really good at spelling.

Are you kidding me? My strength is... that I can spell?

I recall taking part in the sixth-grade spelling bee and coming in second after misspelling the word *suede*.

Besides, a lot of people can spell. That's not a skill. It's just, you know, a thing. So I'm a good speller. Big fucking deal.

What am I supposed to do with this information?

I didn't have the answer to that question. I truly did not know what to do with that information, if it could even be considered information in the first place.

Desperate to learn something useful, I joined an online networking group designed to help freelancers establish themselves and their businesses. One day, I read a post from another group member. In it, she talked about how she had moved from a bustling metropolis on the East Coast to Key West. As a freelancer she could work from anywhere, so she chose the southernmost point in the continental United States. And now she works out of her home, or on the beach, or wherever suits her. She spends her days editing and proofreading materials for clients.

TALK ABOUT A DEFINING MOMENT! I immediately identified with this person. Excitement rushed over me. If I could sit somewhere all day with a huge stack of papers in front of me, red pen in hand, and edit, I'd be in heaven!

Now, a lot of people think I'm crazy when I say that, including my husband, who says he'd go stark-raving mad if that's what he had to do. But that's what makes the world go 'round. Everybody's into different things.

After that realization, I started reflecting on other defining moments in my life. Moments where I had denied myself the opportunity to do that thing that I now realize I love to do and was meant to do. One of those moments occurred shortly after I finished college. With my degree in mass communications, I had secured a position with a local television station. It wasn't exactly what I wanted to do, and the pay wasn't great, but at least it was in my field. I kept an eye out for other opportunities though, and soon I found an opening with a local publishing company in search of a proofreader. I applied for that position. I interviewed for that position. I was offered that position.

I declined that position.

Why? Several reasons, really. The pay was low, lower than what I was making at the television station. It was also a second shift, working from 2 p.m. to 10 p.m. Monday through Friday. Those aren't good hours for someone in their early twenties with a social life. And I had received some input from friends and family who thought I should stay in the broadcast field because that's what my degree was in. So I stayed in broadcasting.

Opportunity missed.

A couple of years later, I was still working in the broadcast field but had moved on from the television station. I saw a job opening at a publishing company. A very well-known publishing company that happened to have an office in my hometown. The position? Salesperson. Anyone who knows anything about me knows that I'm *not* a salesperson. I applied anyway. And I got an interview. At one point during the interview, the interviewer looked directly at me and asked, "Would you rather work in editorial?"

"No," I replied.

I wanted her to believe me. She didn't. She could see in me what I couldn't or what I was denying myself. She knew I wasn't right for the sales position, and I didn't get the job. I also didn't get a job in their editorial department because I refused to be honest with myself and with the interviewer.

I denied myself that opportunity, right there on the spot, by answering, "No."

REFLECTING ON THOSE MOMENTS—THE spelling bee, the proofreading job, the publishing job, the instant connection with a freelancer who was doing what I wanted to do—led me to my truth. I discovered what I had been denying myself for so long:

I can spell.

Spark:

I can spell because I've been a voracious reader since I was a young child. I always read books above my grade's reading level. I looked forward to visits from the bookmobile at school, and I anxiously awaited summer so I could participate in the local library's summer reading program. English was always my favorite subject, from grade school through college. I inhaled the crisp aroma of brand-new textbooks. I've always been passionate about reading and words and language.

Yes, *I can spell!*

THROUGHOUT MY CAREER, I was often the go-to person to review materials before they were finalized and sent to print or distributed, even though none of my positions ever included the words *editor* or *proofreader* in their titles. All these defining moments were showing me the way forward. I just needed to figure out how to take those first steps.

I joined a local networking group and started getting my name out in the open to drum up business. I connected with other freelancers in my online group and offered free editing services to one of the people in the group who had written a short work of fiction. This was something I could use to build my portfolio.

My first manuscript edit! Go me!

I enrolled in a professional certificate program to learn more about manuscript editing. The program took a little more than a year to complete and was worth every penny. I learned a lot in that program that helped me become a better writer and editor. I also unlearned a lot of things I had convinced myself were right about grammar as well as relearned some things I likely first learned in seventh grade or things I had completely forgotten.

Once I accepted my truth and decided where to focus my business to help others, the universe expanded. It heard me and agreed with my assessment. The stars aligned and the clients appeared. Not wanting to let the universe down, I continued to pursue opportunities to learn more about writing, editing, and publishing so I could gain the knowledge needed to further help my clients achieve their goals of becoming published authors.

To this day, I seek out opportunities for growth in my writing and editing. By consistently working to improve my craft and expand my knowledge base, I can provide more and higher-quality services to my clients. I started out offering basic writing services for blogs and websites. That led to offering manuscript evaluation and editing services, then to ghostwriting nonfiction, then to book coaching.

All because *I can spell.*

Those three words—*I can spell*—mean so much more than an ability to spell words correctly. Those words are at the core of my being. They represent my love for books and reading and writing. They are my truth.

OUR DEFINING MOMENTS ARE SIGNALS. We need to take time to reflect on them and determine what they're trying to tell us. One of my defining moments crushed me, but it led to enlightenment about my purpose. I turned my failure—failure to recognize my own worth, failure to accept my true calling, failure to believe in myself—into a flourishing career. A career I'm passionate about and excited to share with others. Now that I know my truth, I'm unstoppable. I'll continue to learn and grow, and to help others realize their dreams in the process.

Through my ghostwriting, editing, and book coaching, I'm able to help my clients identify some of their defining moments. Getting to the core of who they are helps them create a better story for their readers. They become more relatable to their audience, and their messages become more impactful as a result.

What are some of your defining moments? If you ask others what they think you're good at, what will they say? And how can you take that information and build on it to create something you're proud of and can share with others? Your talents are a gift when you're able to share them with others to help them realize their potential.

I love to help my clients achieve those lightbulb moments, when all the puzzle pieces fall into place, and they see the path forward. If your dream includes publishing a book to establish yourself as an authority in your field, attract more clients, secure more speaking engagements, or leave a legacy, reach out. Together we can identify your defining moments—the messages you want to share with your audience—and craft a book that will position you as an industry thought leader.

I can spell. What can you do?

JENNY WATZ

Jenny Watz is the owner of Write Ambitions and works with authors, businesses, and leadership professionals to help them tell their stories in impactful ways. As a communications professional with more than 20 years of experience working with varied industries and diverse audiences, she provides her clients with a unique perspective on how to craft their messages. Jenny edits both fiction and nonfiction manuscripts, ghostwrites nonfiction, and provides book writing and accountability coaching to leadership professionals and independent authors. She is the creator of the online course, Lit at Lunch: 27 Days to Write and Publish Your Book, and is the author of Book Your Biz! How to Use the Book Compass Method to Attract More Clients and Build Your Business. When she's not reading, writing, or editing, Jenny loves spending time with her husband and their hound dog and volunteering with local pet rescue organizations.

linktr.ee/writeambitions

SPARKING GENIUS
BY ADRIENNE MACIAIN, PHD

It all started with the avocado tree that bore no avocados.
Like that tree, I was feeling fruitless in every aspect of my life.

My master's defense had been an absolute blood-bath that left me openly weeping and apologizing for wasting everyone's time.

Truthfully, though, that apology had been aimed at one person only: my advisor, Catherine.

CATHERINE HAD GONE OUT on a limb and convinced the department to give me a full-ride fellowship to study traditional West African performance, her own area of expertise. I wanted desperately to be the protege she could point to with pride, but I was no longer the person I had been when I applied to the program. Something within me had shifted. Or rather, something had broken. Something that would take a very long time to heal.

Which brings me to my equally fruitless marriage. Those who've read *Melting Ivory* know that I was married to a West African man whose latent abusive and narcissistic tendencies had, under culture-shock-induced pressure, exploded into full bloom.

School was my only escape from what I can only describe as constant psychological torture, so when it came to my research, the last thing I wanted to do was watch videos of my tormentor performing with the troupe we'd met in back in Abidjan.

In fact, anything even tangentially related to my ostensible area of study would set off anxiety/panic attacks, followed by shame, self-loathing, and outright catatonia. I would often find myself in the library, staring out the window, or even at the wall, feeling like my body was made of lead; unable to move, having no idea how long I had been there or how to snap myself out of it.

I didn't have the words, or rather the letters, to describe it at the time, but in retrospect it's a pretty clear-cut case of PTSD.

Against that backdrop, auditioning for the undergrad production of Big Love and signing up for Naomi Iizuka's playwriting class looks a lot like a desperate attempt to reclaim my missing mojo.

I thought getting back to my comfort zones of creative writing and performing would provide a much-needed confidence boost. I fancied myself the experienced ringer amongst the undergrad amateurs, and looked forward to soaking up the spotlight and raking in the applause.

Instead, I was consistently shown-up by the fresh-faced talent surrounding me, and at every turn felt blocked, stymied, left-out, and devastated by the tepid reception my disappointing output received.

The worst part was that I couldn't even blame them. Everything I did felt contrived, inauthentic, calculated to impress, and all of it backfired unspectacularly.

That is, until the spark.

It happened one night after rehearsal. As usual, I was unlocking my bike as slowly as possible, stretching out that precious liminal time between school and home, when I was exceptionally authorized to be no place in particular.

That's when I heard a voice call out from behind me.

It was the very voice, saying the very words I had been secretly hoping to hear for weeks: that of the unreasonably cute boy I had been cast opposite—we'll call him "Luke"—imploring me to "Wait up!"

I'm not gonna lie: this was an invitation no part of me wanted to decline.

I did my best to act casual as we chatted about nothing while Luke unlocked his bike, and as we rode side-by-side through the moonlit streets of Isla Vista, listening to the waves pounding against the beach, just a few blocks to the left, and breathing in the cool, salty evening air.

All too soon, we reached the house where Luke lived with multiple undergraduate dudes like himself.

This, I knew, was my cue to say goodnight and keep riding on home. Home to grad student housing. Home to my husband who was surely already livid at my lateness.

Instead, I pivoted, turning my bike in a large, lazy circle from sidewalk to sidewalk and asked him, because it was the only thing I could come up with on short notice, about the tree in front of his house.

"Is that an avocado tree?"

"Yep," Luke replied, circling in the opposite direction and reaching out to playfully kick my tire as he passed.

"Then why doesn't it have any avocados on it?"

I WAS PAINFULLY aware that everything about this situation was wrong. I was a Ph.D. candidate pushing thirty, teaching classes to kids Luke's age. And if my husband could see this tension-laden tableau, he would automatically jump to the conclusion my own mind was struggling to avoid.

But at the same time, there was something touchingly innocent about the scene. Two grown-ass adults acting like adolescents, riding our bikes like binary stars in orbit, wondering how long we could get away with this before the inevitable intrusion of reality.

"Because," he sang out in the universal cadence of I-know-something-you-don't-know, "there's only one tree."

"So what?" I laughed, reaching out to kick his tire and missing.

"Sooooo," he smirked, gliding into a figure-eight, "avocado trees cross-pollinate; you need at least two trees to grow avocados."

Click.

Just as Luke finished saying the word "avocados," the streetlamp overhead clicked off, leaving us in darkness.

And there it was: the spark.

That night, after the requisite brow-beating, I stayed up late writing the first scene of what would eventually become the only play I've written to ever be produced: *Spark*.

Spark is a quirky, off-beat, darkly comic coming-of-age tale involving involuntary electromagnetism, sexual awakening, and of course, an avocado tree.

But that first scene was just a couple of kids, riding their bikes in binary circles, talking about nothing. Two humans enjoying the liminal space between school and home, between childhood and puberty, between the fluid and the fixed, the unspoken and the explicit.

SOUR: I think there's a poltergeist in my house.

SPARK: Forreal?

SOUR: Yeah. S'fuckin' creepy, Dude. [...] It's, like, obsessed with the number two.

SPARK: What?!

SOUR: Yeah, man. I'll be playing on the computer, and all the sudden, the'll be all these twos filling up the screen, like somebody's finger is pushing on the two key, only my hands are on my lap, right?

SPARK: So you need a new computer. That doesn't mean / you have a poltergeist.

SOUR: That's how it started, but now it's spread. So I'll be in the kitchen, like, pouring a bowl of, like, Frosted Flakes or whatever, and all the sudden I hear this "beep, beep, beepbeepbeepbeepbeep" coming from the microwave. And when I look over, the little timer screen is just solid twos.

SPARK: Isn't that dangerous? I mean, what if somebody hit start on accident and there was nothing in there? Don't microwaves like, blow up when that happens?

SOUR: Yeah, man! That happened to my friend's cousin once. Sparks flyin' everywhere and like radioactive shit zapping the whole fuckin' house. Probably everyone on that whole block is, like, sterile now.

I KNEW from the moment I heard it read aloud that I was on to something. And not just because it got laughs. It resonated with me on a frequency I hadn't felt in a very long time: *desire*.

No, not for Luke. I mean, yeah, definitely for Luke, but not *just* for Luke. I had tapped into a soul-level longing for *intimacy*, for genuine connection with another human being. One who would embrace my vulnerability instead of brandishing it like a weapon to be used against me at every available opportunity.

Like so many attractive youths throughout history, Luke had acted as a muse, sparking genius in me just by sharing his authentic energy.

But unlike the artists of antiquity, I didn't feel the drive to possess my muse so I could keep feeling that spark. I understood something they apparently didn't: the flame was in me all along. Luke was just the friction that re-ignited it.

This is what people do for one another, intentionally or otherwise. Whether they rub us the right way or the wrong way, either way they supply the necessary grit to light up the match we always were.

Like avocado trees, our creativity cross-pollinates. But forget the sanitized, kumbaya version of collaboration you've been sold. More often than not, sparking genius involves clashing and crashing and tension and discomfort. Egos are bruised, unmet needs are surfaced, and we are confronted with the opportunity, as powerful as it is painful, to silence our scarcity story and tap into "something beyond ourselves," a.k.a. Source energy.

And tap in, I did.

Grateful as I was to Luke, I no longer lingered after rehearsal in hopes of hearing his plaintive "Wait up!" Instead, I rode home with my new friends, these delightfully flawed characters who had so openly revealed themselves to me, down to the most awkwardly intimate of details, and who accepted and embraced me exactly as I was in return.

But even as I eavesdropped on and transcribed their conversations, I knew it was my own emotional truth I was channeling through their voices. That's why Spark succeeded where all my other efforts had failed. Born of a genuine desire to connect, it was *authentic*. And that authenticity began to spread across my life in exciting and dangerous ways.

I started to take more risks.

IT WAS SUBTLE AT FIRST. A bold choice in rehearsals here, a quirky comment in class there. But it felt so fucking good to say YES to my intuition that my experimentation quickly gathered momentum. I found myself gravitating to new topics, things I had never allowed myself to consider before because there was no obvious connection to West Africa.

By the time I realized I had fallen in love with a completely different, totally uncharted area of study (youth culture and the U.S. Carnivalesque) and would need to shift my entire concentration and therefore switch to a new advisor, it was already too late.

Having gotten a taste of the lit-up life, there was no stuffing that genie back in the bottle.

But contrary to the dire predictions of my anxiety, Catherine did not call me an ungrateful wretch, revoke my fellowship, and banish me from the program. Quite the opposite: she beamed at my newfound enthusiasm and gave me some of the best career/life advice I've ever received:

"Follow the fire," she told me. "Without the fire, you won't finish."

I felt the truth of this on an almost molecular level. The last thing the world needed was another ABD ("All-But-Dissertation") struggling to write another passionless paper solicited by no one.

That tore it. I was all-in. This girl was on fire.

My time in the library was no longer spent staring at the wall, but pawing gleefully through the archives, poring over resource materials (including, for reasons I won't get into here, an entire decade of Playboy magazines), and writing, writing, writing like I'd never written before.

Jody, the notorious "dragon lady" whose pointed questions had reduced me to tears at my Master's defense, asked me to read one of my chapters aloud in class. When I'd finished, she turned to the class and said, "Now *that* is an academic paper."

But where there's fire, someone's bound to get burned.

As things at school heated up, things at home veered into the surreal.

At first I could dismiss the odd occurrences as an amusing coincidence. Streetlamps clicking off just as I rode or walked past them. Numbers popping up on my laptop screen that I definitely hadn't typed there.

"Ha! Just like in the play," I would chuckle to myself.

But then one night when I was up late grading papers, I heard the microwave beep. That was curious because my husband A. was asleep in the bedroom and B. did not cook.

At first I ignored it, but then I heard it beep again. And again.

I walked into the kitchen to see the number "1:11" on the digital display.

As I stood there, agog, it beeped one more time.

11:11

I stared at those numbers for a very long time before pushing "clear/off." And when I did, it just happened to be exactly 11:11 P.M.

For weeks after that, I would wake up from a dead sleep, or feel the impulse to look up from my work, only to see 11:11 on the clock.

That synchronicity was a bridge too far. It had to mean *something*. But what?

Of course, deep down, I knew exactly what it meant: that if I continued down this path of trusting my fire, it would eventually light up every aspect of my life and burn this shitshow of a marriage to the ground. In fact, I knew damn well that the fuse had already been lit and that I should run before the powder keg blew.

But knowing a thing, and doing a thing, are two different things.

I won't spoil the ending except to say that his wife did not survive that explosion. But like a phoenix from that flame, a version of me I never knew existed, one who took the microwave's advice and looked out for number one, was born.

GROWING UP TAKES TIME, though. It took me longer than I care to admit to transition fully into self-trust, and truthfully it's still a work-in-progress. But I allowed that flame, albeit in a slow, controlled burn, to melt down and reform every detail of my existence. And I would do it all again. Only faster, and more gleefully.

By deliberately partnering with my own intuition, I discovered an even more fundamental form of creative cross-pollination: co-creation with Source.

By the time I graduated (with honors), not only was I happily divorced, I was a published author, a produced playwright, and a celebrated teacher and researcher.

In contrast to my indefensible Master's defense, my PhD defense was an outright lovefest, with the department chair calling my dissertation "brilliant," Naomi Iizuka calling it "an absolute delight," and my advisor high-fiving me repeatedly.

Still, it would be a couple more decades (and marriages, and careers) before I was ready to recognize and embrace my true calling: to help others realign to Source, spark genius by tapping into authentic desire, and co-create to innovate with ease and enjoyment.

I write this in hopes that you can shave a decade, a career, or a marriage or two off of your own journey to self-trust. Consider this your formal invitation to stop judging your desires and start prioritizing them NOW.

You deserve to live life lit up. And believe me: your flame is in there. It's always been in there. Burning bright. Ready and waiting to transform your life, if you're willing to light the spark.

ADRIENNE MACIAIN, PHD

Adrienne MacIain, PhD is a creative living coach and bestselling author. She helps those suffering from creative burnout to spark genius with ease & enjoyment so they can SHINE their authentic gifts out to the world, simply by realigning them to Source energy and unleashing the power of their natural creative rhythm, the "DOER" cycle.

linktr.ee/adriennemaciain

PERMISSION FOR PLEASURE
BY ELIZABETH CARTAGENA

We can say that we don't have the best relationship with our own bodies, there is always something we want to change. It is an endless cycle that is hard to break. There is also a false acceptance that we try so hard to convince ourselves it is real. I thought I had a great relationship with my body, I thought I loved my body, until I had a breakthrough with bodywork that I had never imagined possible.

BEFORE THE BREAKTHROUGH, the shame I felt in my body remained hidden, even from me.

I was 15 years old when I started exploring my sexuality, kissing boyfriends and some hot grinding moments with clothes in the house. Then I felt like falling in love with Juan, my boyfriend for 5 years with whom I started my genital sexuality (the phrase "I lost my virginity" should be eliminated from our speech). After breaking up with him, I explored my sexuality with many other men. Friends with benefits, one-night-stands, and many more experiences that I felt I needed to explore. So that gave me some confidence to talk about sex with my friends.

For a friend's bachelorette party, we hired a woman to teach us sexy dancing. She did some games and questions, and I won them all. We became friends, and she invited me to a tantra event.

I agreed and went, with the sole intention that I wanted to learn to start sharing the information and working in this field.

We traveled to the city for the weekend workshop. There were like 20 people, couples and single men and women. Everything was going smoothly, with breathwork and meditations, until it came time for massage and we all had to get naked. Panic attack activated!

I STARTED SEEING everyone around naked and then thinking I had to take my clothes off. All I could think was, "What will these other people think when they see me naked?"

In that moment, I realized I was all talk: my confidence around sex was a scam, my mind had tricked me into thinking that I could do this sex confidence thing easily with friends and partners, but when it came to another scenario like a transformational workshop, that confidence flew away.

I was back in my room, changing and gathering the elements they asked for at the workshop, thinking of two choices left at that moment: flee from the opportunity, or stay and remember the intention. That is when everything fell into place, the moment I gave myself the permission to go out there in front of people in my naked body with my nervous soul. That was the deciding moment.

I WAS able to do the exercise, but afterwards I felt like I had climbed a mountain. After two days of hard work of meditations, breathwork and massage our teacher in the workshop asked for a volunteer to demonstrate the yoni massage (vagina with power).

Picture all of us, 20 people sitting in a circle, and the teacher asking for a woman volunteer to come into the circle to demonstrate how to do it. My right hand immediately raised by itself, the rest of my body stayed there in panic, questioning what my right hand was doing. I mean, two days ago I arrived at the workshop nervous and couldn't show my body naked, and now I wanted to be in the center of everybody, getting a yoni massage.

THERE WAS DEFINITELY something pushing me that was not me, but all for good. It was the best thing that has ever happened to my body. The relationship with my body changed completely.

The massage started applying all the techniques we learned, both from her side, and my side. I forgot that there were people there, I started elevating myself with my breath and her hands, my head towards the back as if I were possessed, until she said, "Put into my fingers all the shame, fear, and abuse from your whole life."

That is when I felt the flame of guilt and shame burning inside me go out. I wasn't there, my soul wasn't there. I know my physical body was, but not me. When I came back to my body, 40 eyes were on me, watching the entire experience. But that didn't matter, because my own spark had just ignited, a spark of pleasure without shame.

I sat down, my body was moving from side to side in perfect equilibrium, I felt I loved everyone, as if I were under the influence of some drug.

SINCE THAT DAY, my relationship with my body is of full trust, no matter what others say or think.

Of course, we don't all have to live this exact experience. But to go from shame to pleasure, there has to be permission involved. The permission you give to yourself, allowing yourself to experiment with your body through movement. Billions of cells that you move to give you a message of life, because your body can perceive things faster than your mind. But because we are so disconnected from it, we forget to pay attention to it.

I heard about an experiment: connecting sensor cables to right and left hands and head for picking cards out of two decks. One deck produced winning cards on and off, the other deck not so often. So, the next time the person thought from which deck to pick a card, the hand had already decided. They could see movement in the right hand before the card was drawn. Meaning the hand was automatically being activated with energy in the cells from what it had already learned, together with the mind that the right deck had more chances of getting winning cards. So, the body is giving you signals first, before the mind. Yet we listen to the mind first because we are very disconnected from our bodies and can't hear the signals they are giving. Pleasure is a way to reconnect with your body.

AFTER THAT LIFE-CHANGING WORKSHOP EXPERIENCE, I started giving myself the permission to explore more of my body and connection to the mind. Years later, I realized how it continued to push me through a path of self-discovery.

I had spent a sabbatical year the year before the workshop; I gave myself the permission to experience uncertainty, quitting the 9-5 job and going to explore the world. This was during my 25th year of life, my life before 25 is gone and I feel. Still, after the workshop, my intention of learning about tantra and sexological body work remained, but I felt it from a whole different perspective. It invited me to check myself first, to get to know myself and then to help others.

I embarked on a journey of self-discovery. I did many different therapies, from tarot, bioprogramation, natal chart, all to understand myself better and get to know myself. But the ones that have marked my life the most have been this sexological bodywork and the game of my ego. This was one of the therapies that definitely changed the way I thought completely. So, if you can picture my map, it started off by giving myself permission to live a different life. I wasn't happy with my life at 23, so I gave myself that permission.

With the same woman that invited me to the workshop, I started to create and host workshops. We did it for almost a year, teaching tantra and other techniques to connect with your body and your pleasure. We stopped working together because I decided to travel again, still studying myself, but when I came back, I did two other formations on pleasure and women's sexuality along with quantum theories for the soul that complimented myself. Combining all of these with the game that Placerologia was born.

PLACEROLOGIA IS a Spanish term for a rough translation of Pleasure-Ology, the permission you give yourself to discover your own pleasure.

Placerologia is now my energetic baby. I think all of this started when I gave myself permission. This is what I really mean by permission, let me tell you the story.

I was trapped in what I call the possible, meaning what your mind thinks is possible, from your own experiences you create this outcome. Back then I was working an 8-5 job, just waiting for the days to pass so I could enjoy the weekend.

I remember one day coming to work and around 10 am I said: Fuck it! Life can't be 8-5 every day. I had been working for the family business for 2 years and I was doing well, but sitting in the office in front of the computer at 24 years old, I knew that wasn't it for me.

Then I began to think: what have I always wanted to do and haven't done yet? What did I really want to do with my life? I was only able to answer the first question back then.

I ALWAYS WANTED to study in another country, live in a real exchange, learn other languages like Portuguese. Many of my good friends in Miami were from Brazil and I always saw them happy. So, I needed to research and understand why they were always happy. That's how I said I want to go to Brazil to live in a real exchange program in another country and learn not only Portuguese but also why they are happy.

So, I made a plan to do a sabbatical year traveling. I had a clear desire, and there I focused all my attention. For 6 months after I made that decision, this desire completely guided my life. I saved money, stayed single, and put up with my job because I knew it was temporary and everything would soon change.

SHED LIGHT ON YOUR DESIRES, and what it will take to fulfill them. It will keep you motivated.

Desires are very different from things you love. I loved my family, but working with them wasn't making me happy, I desired traveling and new experiences.

So, when my passport arrived, I did what I had to do: I ended my apartment lease. I sold my car. I cut a lot of expenses like internet, TV, and meal plans. And I quit the job.

After I gave notice, something happened.

Everything was ready for my sabbatical year. So, I threw a farewell party with close friends and coworkers. We drank and danced, and I cried. There was a coworker who was hitting on me, but I didn't give a damn about him.

The next day I went to the office, and I still felt dizzy. The days went by and I didn't sleep, I didn't eat, I didn't know what was happening to me. I began to suspect that this coworker had drugged me and that's why I was like this. When I went to the hospital, they didn't find any substance and they said it was a panic attack. I realized that I was very hesitant to take this leap of faith into the unknown.

However, I went ahead with my plan, and things fell into place and flowed divinely. It was a year that changed my life completely.

IT TAUGHT me the strength I have to fulfill what I really want and from then on, my life has always been full of desires and of pure enjoyment. Having a clear desire as a goal, observing what obstacles can come up and also emotions making you blame others like I thought I was drugged when it was really fear invading my mind. I was able to overcome all of this and accomplish my goal.

Part of empowering ourselves starts by connecting with our roots and honoring them through the development of these powerful qualities. To give birth is not only about the act of bringing a baby into this world, but rather to create something tangible that comes from our desires and ideas; this is what we refer to as manifestation. This is what I did with Placerologia.

PLACEROLOGIA IS MY BABY, my business. In the beginning I compared myself to the friend I started with and other people that were doing something similar and I couldn't advance. Then when I remembered to see my business as my baby, I gave it space, I stopped comparing it and let it take the steps needed for its development. Meaning it will learn how to walk once it has crawled.

Some days, I wanted to let it go and work on something else, but then I remembered it was my baby. Will I quit on it now that it can still have potential but is just my mind playing games with it? So I continue, those obstacles can be either internal or external, I call them sphinxes, like the one in Egypt is right in front of the pyramids protecting what is sacred. You can find them in many places and temples, like an ugly dragon preventing you from reaching the most sacred thing.

Placerologia is my baby and my sacred thing. I give meaning to it based on how I think about it, how I talk about it and how I feel about it. My dream is that my energetic baby grows to a certain age that can then live on its own, that it can relate to other people that share the same vision. A vision in which men and women can be connected with their own pleasure, that they give themselves the permission to feel pleasure and change the belief that to achieve something in life it has to be done with pain.

Placerologia has given me the chance to work with amazing women and help them in their own journey of overcoming shame and guilt to reach a pleasurable state, not only physically but also mentally and emotionally. Because everything is connected. Maybe you don't know what shame or guilt you carry, reducing your capacity to feel pleasure. I can teach you a way to find out.

Spark:

Not by looking at this specific area of your life, but by looking at the bigger picture.

TELL me how you are in sexuality and I'll tell you how you are at work. Or tell me how you are at work, and I'll tell you how you are in sexuality. No, I'm not a psychic (although we women really are, with our great intuitive sense), but I understand that wellness is holistic.

See, we tend to divide our life in an imaginary sense. We have different areas in our life and we think that in each of them we behave differently, have different rules, and have different thought processes.

Take a look at the graphic below, you probably have seen it before. Those are the main areas in which we tend to classify our life. It's like a pizza divided into 8 slices.

How is your relation with...

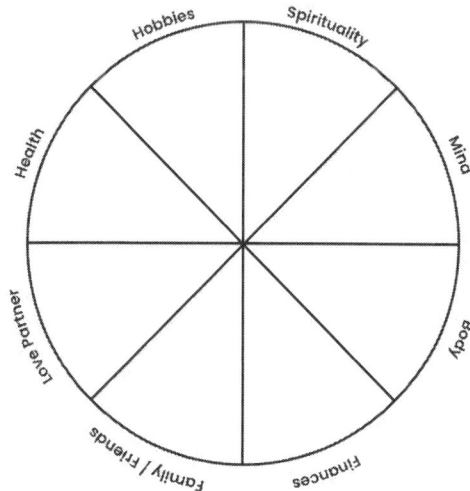

Here I invite you to rate each slice of the pizza from 1-5. After marking all the numbers, pick the one that is lowest. If for example your finances are at the lowest slice, being at a 1 or 2, and you want it to be at 4 or 5, then look at the opposite in the chart.

IF YOU TRACE a line passing through the center, it means one is connected with the other. Look at it regarding the energy you spend on each slice. For example, how much energy you dedicate to the Love Partner slice talks about how the energy you have towards your Spirituality and vice versa, because it is the fact that you believe in your spirituality that allows you to share love with your partner, like a mirror. Another way to see it is that if you focus positively on one slice like your hobbies, then your finances can improve.

Our true self is that point in the middle from which you observe your reality outside. That point in the middle is from where your psychic world is governed. That's where the magic happens, and you can go from shame to pleasure in all your areas.

ELIZABETH CARTAGENA

Elizabeth Cartagena is the creator of Placerologia, certified in Taoist Tantric Massage and Quantum Energy for the benefit of being, trained in Pleasure and Female Sexuality.

Traveling was her passion and her old job was obstacle. She went on a journey that led her to leave a corporate life for a career to create Placerologia / Pleasurology as a service for women to recognize their own pleasure. On her inner journey she invested in a lot of knowledge, therapies, workshops, training, etc. At that time only seeing that it was her own desire to know herself. But then she found herself sharing what had worked for her and created something new. Her personal journey now is informing her work to help women connect with their pleasure.

linktr.ee/placerologia

UNLEASHING WOMEN IN LEADERSHIP

BY DR. HYND BOUHIA

My own leadership story started in my family's living room in Casablanca, where my professors convinced my parents to enroll me in the top engineering school in France, instead of staying home and getting married, the traditional route for Moroccan daughters. I knew leaving Morocco would come with many challenges, including the personal pressure I felt for not conforming to my culture's expectations. However, I left for France believing in my grandmother's words. I could create my own life. One beyond the restrictions laid out for me. It's not that I didn't care about my family's wishes, but I knew I would be a better daughter, friend, and human following my own path.

During my doctoral studies at Harvard and later on at Johns Hopkins, even during my stint working at the World Bank, my grandmother's words of encouragement kept me focused on what I could achieve.

This was the beginning of my global life.

I sought excellence in whatever I did. I worked harder, longer hours and proved to myself every day that university was the right decision. Even when my male peers criticized me, saying women were too soft or too weak to make it in the business world, I was determined to honor myself and develop the needed skills to make business a welcoming place for women.

MANY GIRLS AND WOMEN, especially in the developing world, need encouragement to reach for their true potential. This is why I utilized the skills I learned in my training to embark on a mission to empower one billion girls and women to grow confident, resilient, tech-savvy and financially free.

We are living in an unprecedented era, where business seems to favor the rise of women in the spotlight. Women are stepping forward to share their gifts with others, leading with great service and sustainable impact.

I asked myself how women in leadership is reflected in the daily realities of women's lives and realized: women in leadership is not just for global superpowers or highly developed countries, it is foundational to each girl and woman looking for examples on how to express their integral purpose in their communities.

After 20 years of experience in development, strategy and finance, I've witnessed firsthand the impact of leadership on communities. Leadership is to be able to influence someone's thoughts, feelings, emotions and actions to empower and inspire positive change.

I've also realized: women are born leaders.

EVERY WOMAN Is **Born A Leader**

Every woman is born with the potential to realize the highest role she wishes to access. She can be a president, an entrepreneur, a leader... so much to aspire to.

Today, women increasingly have options. They can choose to embark on diverse careers and advance as far as their innate capacity and hard work will carry them. Women can attain leadership and decision-making positions, not just by piling up advanced degrees, but also by launching successful ventures and innovative products.

So, what holds women back?

The environment a girl grows up in can largely influence how she shows up in the world. If she is told, "girls can't do that," she will have a difficult time realizing her innate potential to contribute to the health and vitality of the workplace. All of this can keep her small, lacking confidence, and drowning in frustration.

What do women need to get themselves out of this vicious cycle? They need role models to inspire them. They need the skills to power up and raise their confidence. They need a support system that ignites their passion for service and for leading. Women need to feel safe, and safe to create a nurturing environment for others.

We Need More Role Models

Whenever a woman holds a position of leadership, power, and intellectual or artistic genius, she inevitably becomes a role model for girls. Beyond personal career achievements, this role feels especially satisfying to those who have overcome so many barriers in their own lives before achieving their dreams.

Many women are the pillars of their family. They help develop the next generation while courageously leading their households. However, the number of women who've made news and marked history with their names have been painfully few.

This only emphasizes the need for professional female role models, inspiring girls to follow their path, stand on their shoulders, and build on their examples. This need runs through all disciplines, but especially in science and technology. 30% of today's scientists are now women. Yet, they still struggle against the male-dominated current. In the hottest fields, like Artificial Intelligence, women do not exceed 13% of the workforce, allowing male-programmed machine learning algorithms to perpetuate gender stereotypes in Big Tech.

However, change is on the horizon.

Crashing The Tech Glass Ceiling

Women have distinguished themselves in leadership roles all over the world and in different fields. When they crashed through the glass ceiling into the technology world, it demonstrated that gender discrimination in business could be a thing of the past. We have acclaimed women CEOs in high-tech companies such as YouTube, Yahoo, and IBM, with similar trends in politics and international organizations. Even finance and banking is catching up. For example, Jane Frazer was nominated as the President of Citigroup and also as the Head of several Stock Exchanges around the world, including the New York Stock Exchange.

Women are reaching high-level positions from the Western world to the Far East. Nevertheless, some countries seem to be more advanced than others.

WHY SOME COUNTRIES Lead In Leadership

Let us begin with one eye on Scandinavia's exemplary leadership. Iceland, Norway, Finland and Sweden have each shown that closing the gender gap is possible. According to the Global Gender Gap report[1], 95% of women in Norway and 86% in Iceland have jobs, compared to the world average of 55%. These countries have women representing on the board of directors, the Venice Commission, and head-of-state leadership. In Iceland, the government established a quota of 40% of women on company boards. In all four countries, women have earned a measure of undeniable equality. In the Global Gender Gap Index, Nordic women rank on top.

By establishing a social safety net, state policies in Nordic countries are especially empowering to women, providing support and generous maternity leave, ensuring a healthy work-life balance, and the freedom to focus equally on personal growth and professional development.

There is a direct correlation between gender gaps and political policies. However, the world is witnessing more women in public positions of leadership, and at increasing rates. Gender gaps close or open due largely to policy, which depends on politics, which in turn depends on politicians. Encouragingly, it is today far more acceptable throughout the world, including in Africa and other developing parts of the world, to see those positions of public leadership filled by women.

The confirmation of the United States' first female Vice President Kamala Harris was a major boost for girls, particularly girls of color, all around the world. Kamala Harris confirmed in her opening speech that she "may be the first woman to hold this office. But (she) won't be the last."[2] She spoke of the women who have "paved the way" for her election.

In April 2012, Malawi's first female president, Joyce Banda, traveled to Liberia to meet President Ellen Johnson Sirleaf, who announced she "is not going to be lonely among men anymore."[3] They were joined two years later by Catherine Samba-Panza, president of the Central African Republic (CAR), and the fourth African female head of state.

Preparing For Leadership Starts Early

When progressive policies are in place, the number of women holding leadership and decision-making positions can rise. At the center of the 2030 United Nations Sustainable Development Goals, countries are striving to meet the gender guidelines. We are seeing more women in executive boards and members of parliaments, as well as in governments.

There are two main areas of growth toward women in leadership. The first is to help and support women reach positions of authority. The second is to prepare today's young girls to be tomorrow's leaders, so that leadership feels natural to them from an early age. Every young girl can grow with the right mindset to take on responsibilities and use her voice to influence and inspire.

Women in leadership is particularly timely for developing countries, where access to quality education is a luxury for a small percentage of wealthy populations. UNICEF calculates that 129 million girls around the world do not have access to education. The numbers are large for countries affected by conflict, but also in countries lacking the infrastructure to help girls go to and stay at school long enough to graduate. The main reason for this is poverty, resulting in schools which do not meet the safety, hygiene, or sanitation needs of girls.

Gender-equitable education systems need to be standardized throughout the world. If this generation has a fight, it is to ensure that every single girl goes to school. With secure access to quality education, each girl has an opportunity to make well-informed decisions about her present and future.

But it doesn't stop there. Access to quality education for girls allows them to mentor others toward eventual community improvement. Joining their voices to what has often been the exclusive domain of men, female leaders can ensure that nations prioritize investments in human rights, social inclusion, and community services, rather than narrowly spending on centralized, top-down infrastructure projects.

More And More Women Are Rising In Politics!

Over the last century, the number of female political leaders has grown. We have seen the rise of Indira Gandhi of India, Benazir Bhutto of Pakistan, Chancellor Angela Merkel of Germany, and Margaret Thatcher of England.

Merkel is living proof that a girl can choose any career she dreams of, including leadership of a country, or even a group of countries.

On May 20, 1965, the National Union of Townsend's Guilds Conference quoted Thatcher as stating: "If you want something said, ask a man; if you want something done, ask a woman."

One of the most powerful women in the U.S., Nancy Pelosi, wields her gavel with an iron hand over the most democratic branch of Congress, the House of Representatives.

In France, Christine Lagarde has led the International Monetary Fund and now the European Central Bank.

Ruth Bader Ginsberg led the United States Supreme Court for three decades while simultaneously fighting for women's equality in the workplace.

Mary Robinson went from being President of Ireland to taking charge of the United Nations Human Rights Commission, and in a 1998 Harvard graduation speech, argued how women's empowerment is a human right.

Bigger Trends In The Entertainment Business

Some women reveal their power outside of politics, and exemplify how a girl of modest means can achieve her dreams. As a host and media entrepreneur and philanthropist, Oprah Winfrey motivates, encourages and inspires millions of women and girls of all races and religions, worldwide. In South Africa, she launched an education and mentoring program for girls, opening the possibility of having a better future and professional career.

Actress, interpreter and entrepreneur, Jennifer Lopez, developed a business empire and created the Lopez Family Foundation to give back.

Angelina Jolie leverages her fame through humanitarian missions as UN Ambassador.

In 2020, Rihanna received the National Association for Advancement of Colored People (NAACP) award for her public service to the poor, especially black women. Rihanna's 2012 Clara Lionel Foundation, named after her grandparents, contributes to the education of African girls.

These celebrities are examples of women designing their own lives. Even if the expectations of celebrities are different than for a girl from Morocco, they demonstrate how each woman can have a positive impact through business in empowering their communities.

In the business world, resilience and belief in your leadership abilities matter most. Being a leader is a choice each woman gets to make in her own life. In my 20 years navigating the male-dominated business and finance industry, owning my space and demonstrating my skills without reservation were paramount to my success. My grandmother's encouragement was always close to my heart and I remembered why I wanted to work hard to become a leader in business.

I have seen the devastation of children barefoot in the snow, no access to hot water, and ill-equipped schools without books, desks, or hygiene products for girls. Every time I had the floor in a business meeting, I remembered why I wanted to work so hard to become a leader with a positive message for women.

But a link was still missing. I didn't want to fit into the male-centered business world. I wanted to change the way business worked for women. I could not find that link until I became a successful entrepreneur, launching and sustaining several long-standing companies. I realized personal success as a CEO, international business reference, and as a nominee for Forbes 100 Most Powerful Women. During this season, I struggled to rise above the constraints of traditional management and learned how to recreate myself again and again to best champion women in business.

My leadership style utilizes courage and perseverance to empower each woman to become a leader in her own life. The most important example I have of doing this is by standing up after getting knocked down. I have not always received encouragement from my male peers, but I remembered how hard I worked and how far I had come. My grandmother's words resonated with me to never give up.

Access To Technology And Embracing Digital Transition Is Essential

In the past few years, the world has quickly changed, becoming reliant on digital commerce technology, Artificial Intelligence, and online networking. The COVID-19 pandemic exacerbated the situation, making e-commerce and digital transactions the main survival recipe for companies and businesses. This trend will carry on as new economic perspectives shape up and bring big hopes to business owners, entrepreneurs, and corporations.

Women need to become tech-savvy to have a leading role in this new business standard. Business has turned digital and technology is at the center of everything we do.

At first, technology can feel intimidating. However, today developers are creating easy to use applications to sell and buy products, to market services, and to have an instant global presence. Not only can women use technology, but we can develop new technologies to create an equitable world.

The rise of Wi-Fi, 3G networks, smart phones, and village internet cafes has leveled the playing field. The connected rural and mountain woman is today as able to access reliable internet as the urban woman. All the countries of the world have an opportunity to be connected. Through access to information and technology, women can understand how the world is developing and how women play an important and increasingly central role in shaping its direction.

Be That Female Leadership-Enabling Spark![4]

Finally, each one of us can be that spark in someone's life. You can lead and positively influence others, whether as a grandmother, a sister, a mother, or a friend, every woman can play a role in amplifying women in leadership.

We can work to raise awareness among each other and carry a unified voice of hope and possibility. Empowerment comes from understanding the need for autonomy, believing each woman can play a role, and believing the importance of every woman's story.

Every woman can encourage another to grow confident in skill, resilient in mind, and embrace leadership roles in family, community, and the global sphere. We each have the potential to go beyond external restrictions and grow our abilities to lead. My grandmother shared her spark with me. I am here to share mine.

Share your spark!

DR. HYND BOUHIA

Dr. Hynd Bouhia helps women leaders make an impact on the world through her BAL method.[1] She is on a mission to make one billion girls and women around the world confident, resilient, tech savvy and financially free. With a Harvard PhD, an Engineering degree from Centrale Paris, Dr. Hynd has accumulated more than 20 years of professional experience in high-level leadership positions. She is the author of the inspirational and women empowerment book *Africa Girl, African Woman*, and was nominated by Forbes among the 100 most influential women and most influential Arab women in Business (2015), and honored as a member of the Johns Hopkins Society of Scholars (2018).

linktr.ee/drhynd

ADVERSITY - YOUR GREATEST GIFT
BY REEM BORROWS

I have no real interest in politics. However, politics played heavily around me in childhood, shaping my worldview. I saw scarcity and prejudice where once there was equity and abundance. Here, I will share some of the leadership lessons I learned early on in life, as well as during my own leadership journey, and how these principles can be applied to all parts of life.

My childhood was beautiful. I was surrounded by a huge extended family full of unconditional love and support. Anywhere I went in the old country, I had my immediate and extended family to count on. I was surrounded by an abundance of joy, love, and genuine hospitality. I had a huge sense of belonging and a deep inner feeling of pure love. I am amazed, looking back, at how strong those feelings were, despite growing up in a system that supported religious and ethnic segregation, and treated the indigenous population as second or third-class citizens at best.

I AM a Palestinian Christian born in the city of Haifa on the Mediterranean shore. My family is from the Galilee region, where

Jesus Christ is from. We are descendants of the first Christians in the world. My Mother was born in Palestine, my grandmother was born in Palestine, my grandmother's mother was born in Palestine, and so on.

I played in the streets of Haifa and Nazareth, where thousands of years ago, Jesus played as a child and walked as a man. Here, he taught people how to love, demonstrated merciful justice, dismantled social and cultural hierarchies, and worked on ending the division and rejection of people based on faith, social status, and ethnicity. In my neighborhood, he started a global movement that was established through pure love, and oneness. These teachings are foundational in my understanding of leadership. I learned that great leadership comes from an open heart, resilience, love, empathy, and a thirst for growth.

I was born in the exact same area as my ancestors, but by then and due to the "Nakba" (the catastrophe) in 1948, we were no longer allowed to call ourselves Palestinian. We were living under a new political regime that did not recognize our people's history or their right to be there. In 1948, and again in 1967, most Palestinians lost their lands, homes, titles, and deeds, if not their lives. To this day, there is a Palestinian refugee crisis.

As of 2019, more than 5.6 million Palestinians were registered with UNRWA as refugees. The term "Palestine refugee" does not include internally displaced Palestinians or many of those now living in the West. The Palestinians living as refugees are scattered all over the "Middle East" with no papers, no rights, no freedom, and no real recognition. Most Palestinians across the world do not have the right to return to their own homeland.

For me, there is no greater pain than the modern-day Palestinian plight. It was born from manipulation, fear, and greed. The voices of competition and injustice are loud, but through healthy leadership, we can find love and peace. It is through this belief in love that I have learned to forge a life full of abundance and acceptance. I believe that being self-aware is the path to great leadership, freedom, peace, and belonging.

In some ways, every single one of us from all over the world is "Palestinian," looking for truth, belonging, freedom, and prosperity. Each of us, regardless of where we're born, have these foundational principles in common.

Growing up, the politics around me seemed to focus on the oppressor and oppressed. Everything was disguised, nothing was as it appeared to be. Everyone had an opinion and believed their fiercely binary view was correct. I now realize that when people spoke, they spoke in absolutes. There was no middle ground or curiosity in another perspective. Today, speaking in absolutes has become even more prevalent. Is it any wonder that we are experiencing even more division and anger worldwide?

The real global pandemic is not COVID-19. The real pandemic is fear and stress. Fear is consuming us. We are seeing the division clearly now. Division and separation in relationships, society, business, and sadly, in leadership. Division can never bring freedom, growth and prosperity.

1ST LESSON IN LEADERSHIP: THE EBB AND FLOW OF LIFE – HOW WILL ADVERSITY DEFINE YOU?

When we lived in Haifa, my mother worked with people from all communities, religions, and ethnic backgrounds. I had an incredible opportunity to meet and befriend amazing people who had overcome so many hardships in life. Some of my own family members were imprisoned for political reasons, and I spent many weekends visiting them. There, we were treated like cattle in gated pens and I quickly learned that I was seen as an outsider in my own land.

During this time, I also met Muhammad at the school my mom worked at in Nazareth. After picking up what he thought was a shiny ball in a football field, a bomb exploded, costing him his sight, one arm, and a leg from the knee down. Despite Muhammad's obvious physical disabilities, he was one of the smartest kids academically, played football like a professional, and played the Durbaki (a traditional drum) with ease. Muhammad's determination and resilience helped shape my attitude towards adversity. I learned that our adversities may define us, but their effects don't necessarily determine how we define ourselves.

Mohammad never saw himself as a victim. When I spoke to my mom, she said to me, "Reem, no matter what happens to you in life, always come from a position of strength and never a position of weakness." In other words, no matter what life throws at you, no matter how hard things get, rise above it and don't ever play the victim. It doesn't mean we can't feel pain, loss, and sorrow. There will be hard times and we will fall. We will feel pain. Pain is inevitable, but words from the Buddha remind me: suffering is a choice.

Muhammad's story and my first lesson in leadership is etched into me for life. I realized that every person who has achieved anything of any significance in life has had to deal with adversity. When adversity comes, how will you allow it to define you? How you answer this question is part of the journey to becoming a great leader.

2ND LESSON IN LEADERSHIP: LOVE OR FEAR – IT'S YOUR CHOICE!

In truth, we only have two emotions: Love or Fear. You can't see either of them, and they both require you to believe in something. However, they derive totally opposite results! Every other emotion we describe fits into either Love or Fear. All our thoughts, our feelings and our behaviors are influenced by whether we choose to come from a place of love or from a place of fear.

I met many Jewish people who became close family friends. They had survived horrendous conditions during WWII and rebuilt their lives as successful and influential public figures in the State. Having experienced hatred first-hand, they dedicated themselves to helping Palestinians wrongly treated by the system. They saw that the oppressed had become the oppressor. Our Jewish family friends were open, helpful and kind. However, many others saw us as a threat to their well-being. They did not believe we belonged to the same land they had been welcomed into and were now claiming as their own. We were treated with contempt.

These family friends taught me that fear and lack of awareness blinded many. They knew, whether in the past or present, that no one "people" had a monopoly on pain and suffering.

They shared that sight is easily obscured when people don't contemplate different perspectives. When you soften your heart and ask questions, the truth shows up. I knew everyone had a story and that people from all walks of life had overcome unfathomable adversity. I noticed a direct connection between overcoming adversity and active curiosity. Overcoming personal or systemic adversity does not have to come at the expense of another human being.

Great leaders keep an open heart and a curious mind. The best form of leadership comes from a place of unconditional love, care, and kindness with strength. Leadership in any other form will only bring short term "wins" at the expense and often exploitation of others.

When you are kind to others, you are kind to yourself. When you exploit others for your own gain, you also hurt yourself in the process. This is because we are all connected. There is no separation. Every thought and every action has a cause and effect. Eventually, everything affects the collective. We are seeing this in local and global organizations. It's not a matter of *if* our thoughts and actions have an impact, it's a matter of *what* impact our thoughts and actions will have on the whole.

Love in all its purity comes when we keep our hearts open regardless of the circumstance. We allow ourselves to feel the pain, keep our hearts open and express ourselves freely. We must not suppress any of it. When we operate from pure unconditional love and an open heart, when we become consciously aware of our fears, paradigms and things that are holding us back, we start to make decisions that benefit everyone.

Conversely, when we operate from a place of fear, we believe that for us to win, someone else must lose. Throughout my 20 plus year career in all levels of leadership, I have witnessed the belief that winning must come at any cost. This creates a scarcity mentality.

In reality, we are all on the same team. Leading with unconditional love, there is abundance for all. An old friend once told me, the reason doors are placed in rooms is so that Egos can be left outside.

3ʳᴅ Lesson in Leadership – Everyone is looking to belong – gratitude and perspective

My family immigrated to Australia in 1983. We lived in Sydney for the first 9 months, then moved to Darwin for 5 years, before moving to Brisbane for 9 years. Twenty-four years ago, I moved to Melbourne, and finally to Sydney. I am Palestinian, and I am also Australian.

Because I moved so much as a kid, the sense of belonging I had in my childhood disappeared. I felt like I didn't belong anywhere, as though I needed to justify who I was and prove my self-worth to be accepted. Each new place I landed, I had to learn the language, overcome cultural and gender expectations, and forge my way through new surroundings. As I easily externally integrated into new environments, internally I felt out of place with my own identity.

The internal pressure to fit in put me in a constant state of fight, flight, or hide mode. When I went back to the old country, I could no longer understand or relate to the segregation and the humiliation of being treated as an inferior, where both my birth and spiritual roots go back to the time of Jesus Christ. I became acutely aware that "my kind" no longer had the opportunities afforded to others.

In Australia, I learned that those with laser-like focus had plentiful opportunities. Australians loved hard workers and, as a family, we worked on integrating quickly into our new culture to become "Australian." My sense of belonging was rooted in a strong work ethic and a willingness to learn. At university, I worked most evenings and even after graduating, held a day and evening job.

On one of my few "off" evenings, a beautiful friend of mine asked me why I worked so hard. Wasn't it time to live my life while I was still young?

To me, working hard *was* living. I had the opportunity to study wherever and whatever I wanted, to work as hard as I wanted, and to strive as far as I wanted with no prejudice or segregation. I combined work with pleasure, earning money, getting promotions, and making a name for myself without having to prove my identity or sacrifice my personal values. I remembered Muhammad and what most Palestinians had to endure in the old country. I was one of the fortunate ones.

And so, the third leadership lesson was born.

Everything is a matter of perspective and gratitude. Rather than focusing on what you don't have, choose to focus on what you do have.

Wayne Dwyer said it best, "When you change the way you look at things, the things you look at change."

I spent so many years feeling like I didn't belong anywhere, but truthfully, I belonged everywhere! Because I moved around so much, I soon realized that everywhere I went, I knew people. They opened their doors to me with hospitality and love.

Fundamentally, we are all looking for the same thing and that is to be happy and to belong. If only we all realized that we don't need to look for happiness or belonging. Happiness is a choice, not an outcome. We already belong, and happiness is in the moment, not in our destiny.

4TH LESSON IN LEADERSHIP – MAGIC, JOY, AND BELONGING HAPPENS OUTSIDE OUR COMFORT ZONE

From that point on, I found an even deeper love for people from all walks of life. I started to understand that people have more in common than not. There is beauty everywhere. My perspective shifted and I was grateful for all the new and uncomfortable situations I experienced in diverse environments. I quickly learned that, regardless of past or present circumstances, each one of us has tremendous potential, so much to give, and ultimately, so much to experience and grow. And that, for me, was when the penny dropped!

The magic of growth happens outside of our comfort zones. Nothing new is created in our comfort zone. By definition, innovation and creativity can only come when we have no idea how to do something and set goals we have never reached before. We must get comfortable being uncomfortable and doing those things that scare us and excite us at the same time.

5ᵗʰ Lesson in Leadership – Unconditional love and oneness are the most powerful leadership traits

Throughout the ages, Toa Dao, Buddha, Jesus Christ, the Prophet Muhammad (S.A.W.A), Mahatma Gandhi, Martin Luther King, Nelson Mandela, Mother Teresa and so many more, all teach the fundamental life principles I learned as a kid.

If we look from within, there is only unconditional love and oneness. The only reason we look for love and belonging externally is because we have allowed ourselves to be consumed by fear and separateness. Whether you're looking from a physical, intellectual, or a spiritual perspective, connection and oneness are at the center.

We each already belong.

Choosing unconditional love can feel like the road less traveled, but ultimately, it always wins. We know that the balance of power and leadership come and go. Everything has a beginning and an end, no exceptions. The only constant is oneness, the connection between all things.

6ᵗʰ Lesson in Leadership – The quality of your Leadership is determined by the quality of your questions

The last time I walked through the streets of my old country, I could feel tension and fear everywhere. Everyone was losing. Until we understand that fear creates scarcity, there will be lack for all involved. Oppressive "leadership" may feel like winning in the moment, but these behaviors will come back to hurt you. In Australia this is known as the boomerang effect - once you throw it out, it must come back to you!

When there is an oppressor and an oppressed, there will never be peace or calmness for either party. The oppressor, over a period of time, will not only hurt the oppressed, but also their own people. The Palestinian crisis is not a 2000-year old conflict. It is a modern-day man-made crisis that could impact us all globally.

This translates easily into the business environment. Long term, operating from a place of fear and the way behavior manifests itself, will impact everyone. You may feel like you are winning short-term through power, manipulation, and backstabbing, but long-term it will not help anyone's efforts.

ASK YOURSELF: What legacy do you want to leave behind? What impact do you want to have? What type of leader do you want to be?

Then ask yourself: Now that I have all this information, what do I do with it? How will I change? How can I follow the path of unconditional love for greater growth?

Step one is self-awareness.

"95% of who we are by the time we are 35 years old, is a memorized set of behaviors, emotional reactions, subconscious habits, hard wired attitudes, and beliefs that function like a computer program."[1] In other words, our behavior is based on our programming.

Imagine an iceberg. Much of our behavior is influenced by our emotions below the surface. The quicker you understand this within yourself, the quicker you will recognize it in others and know how to respond from a place of understanding.

BECOME A STUDENT OF YOUR SELF! Welcome and allow the truth and pain to surface. Open your heart and, in so doing, pain will dissolve. Pain turns into suffering because we suppress our feelings instead of expressing them. Living from a space of love instead of fear allows caring behavior to live above the surface of the iceberg.

Take a look at the following table and iceberg diagram. Pinpoint your current feelings, based on your behavior.

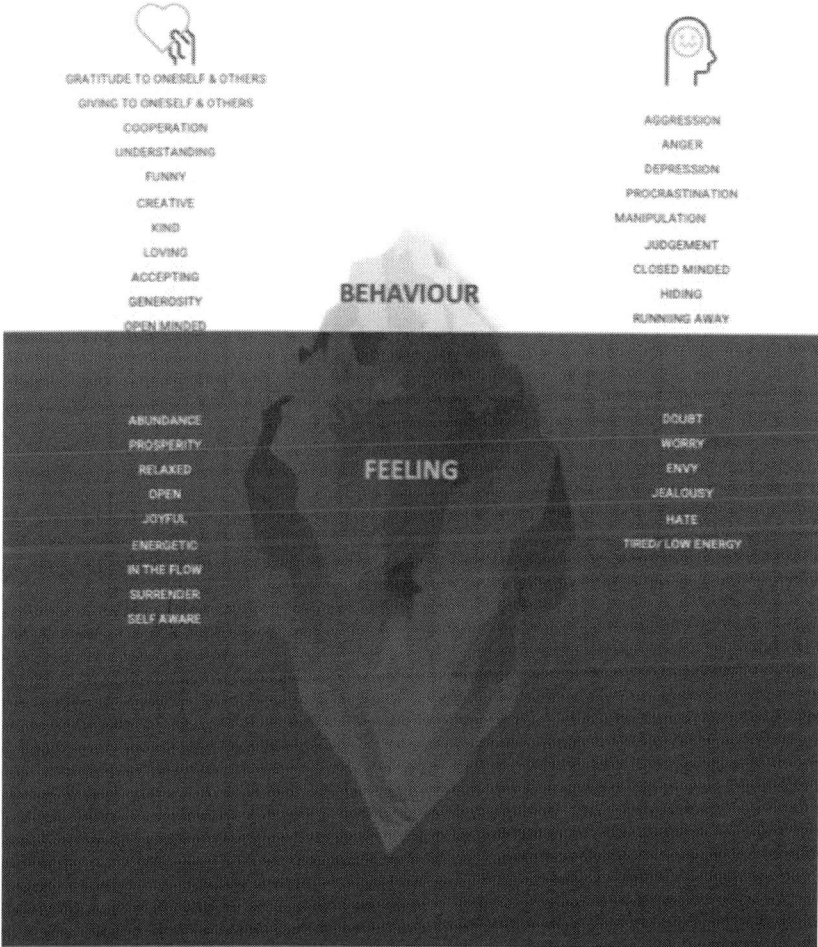

Guided by your feelings, **ask yourself, "Is this coming** from a place of fear or love?"

Unconditional Love	FEAR
Joyful	Aggression
Giving to oneself and others	Jealousy
Grateful for oneself and others	Anger
Cooperative	Envy
Understanding of oneself and others	Manipulation
Open	Low Energy
Adventurous	Blame
Restful	Anxiety
Funny	Sleeplessness
Creative	Being closed-minded
In the Flow	Scared
Relaxed	Doubt
Energetic	Worry
Caring	Procrastination
Kind to oneself and others	Perfectionism
Abundance	Addiction
Prosperperity	Hate
Loving towards oneself and others	War
Accepting of oneself and others	Judgment

Allow yourself to feel **your feelings, ask questions,** and sit in stillness. Over time, you will find yourself shifting towards love because that is our natural state of being. We have an abundant amount of energy for love, as it is aligned with our purpose, and a very limited amount for fear.

SOME POWERFUL QUESTIONS TO PONDER:

- Is this what I want to believe?
- How else can I look at this? What am I not seeing?
- Who can help me see it more clearly?
- What if it could be easy?

- What evidence do I have to prove this?
- How do I want to feel?
- What if I could do it?
- What do I want?
- Is this coming from Love or Fear?
- What is my behavior telling me?
- What are my feelings telling me?
- Who do I want to be in relation to this "situation"?

Conscious awareness of our own feelings and behavior will be the game changer for you, me, and the world. If you want to live free, grow, and become the quality leader you wish to be – if you want to live in prosperity, joy, and abundance, ask yourself one further question.

"WHAT WOULD UNCONDITIONAL LOVE DO?"

This is the single most powerful personal and leadership question you can ask yourself. Every decision you make from there will be the right decision. Will you choose unconditional love, or will you choose fear to guide your decisions and behavior? Unconditional love is the most powerful force created. It eliminates fear and considers the best for everyone, knowing we are all connected.

You can choose to lead in Love. Follow that path regardless of the political, social, or cultural constraints around you. Allow the self-limiting barriers to come down and lead with equity and aspiration.

Here's to Dreems Beyond Borders, to living in a world of abundance.

Dreams do come true.

REEM BORROWS

Human Performance Specialist

For over 20 years, Reem has worked in Senior Leadership Roles leading and developing effective teams and individuals across Sales, Marketing, and Training. Today, she uses her knowledge and expertise to help people realize their full potential in both business and personal goals.

Reem's authenticity as a leader, her business acumen, mindset development strategies, and her dedication to achieving results are the foundations of her work. As a Human Performance Specialist, Reem provides corporate leaders, business owners, and professional individuals with the necessary leadership strategies, training, and mindset to forge new pathways towards meaningful and sustainable growth. Immobility and stagnation can bring about the failure of any good business and career. Reem helps leaders design their own trajectories of positive change and achievement through balance, focus, and flow. These changes have an enormous positive impact on the teams and people around them.

linktr.ee/ReemBorrows

MAKING LEMONADE FROM LEMONS
BY JOSEPHINE S. N. KALAGIRA

Hey Sunshine! My name is Josephine, also known as the Comeback Queen. A strong Christian believer, I currently live in the United Kingdom, but I was born and raised in Uganda.

I AM a proud single mother to Jayden, a special boy of 10 who has not only inspired me to embark on this journey of desiring to make an impact in the world, but also has been the focus of becoming the best version of myself and not giving up despite all the challenges life has thrown at us. He is my reason, why I do what I do.

Is it strange that I am sharing this with you? Oh well! It puts a smile on my face, so let me spill the beans ha ha.

When I was in high school, my two older sisters were both training to become teachers. I thought I could never be a teacher because I believed that you had to have extra-special skills, look and behave a certain way, and be fluent in English speaking and writing. For this reason, I disqualified myself from thinking about being one ever.

In addition, I used to feel shy and embarrassed to speak or hear myself speak out loud. But guess what? I am now where I never thought possible: sharing my story, mentoring, coaching, speaking, writing and hosting global live summits. I keep pinching myself to ensure I am not sleeping so I do not wake up from this dream.

Does this resonate with you too? Please tell me I am not the only one!

Anyway, I keep talking about my wonderful son everywhere I go because he means the absolute world to me. He is my life.

I had Jayden in January 2012, and in September 2012, I chose to go back to university after putting it off for some time. Upon welcoming my son into this beautiful world, he looked so gorgeous and adorable, I knew I wanted to be more and do more so I could be the mum he deserves and can be proud of. I found childcare for him and I committed myself to pursuing a degree in business management and human resources management and graduated after 3 years.

I WAS SO happy and proud. I knew that was the start of our brighter future. I immediately secured a temporary role within the same university before I moved on and worked within a few corporate roles. However, in April 2017, just two months after I had started to settle into my dream role, something tragic occurred and changed everything that I had hoped for.

I remember planning out my life on a vision board, not knowing or considering that in the creation or visualisation mode of our lives, there can also be mitigating circumstances. This can happen to you: your loved one or friend may fall ill, you may lose a loved one unexpectedly, lose a job, a relationship, or have a life-changing condition. We do not usually want to talk about this nor do we want to envision it, but it is reality.

THE QUESTION IS: when tragedy strikes, what do you do? How do you behave? Who do you speak to? How do you know that they will support you? At what point do you start to open up when you are struggling? How do you say it without holding yourself back? Or will you try to keep it contained indefinitely?

These questions create some curiosity, huh? Reality check!

How do you feel about owning and communicating your personal story with confidence? What comes up for you right now? Be honest with yourself, for it is at this point you clearly think and realise whether you are tired of being tired so you can seek to find the right help and support tailored to you. I know this because I totally got it when I was going through challenges and someone told me that, actually, if you want to be better than yesterday, you should always remember that closed mouths do not get fed. This was an eye opener to taking ownership of my life. I hope it speaks to you too.

Looking back on how much personal development and growth I have gone through and what I continue to do, I see that I used to just go with the flow. What others said, I felt. A people pleaser, I was never that kind of person who would question or research thoroughly into anything. I hope this is not you, but if it is, you need to take action now.

I never ever quite understood how people really felt when they are stressed, depressed or struggling with symptoms of anxiety until it hit me. I do not want this for you. I believe this was because I had never turned inward and checked myself on a much deeper level. I was never much into self-discovery. To be honest, I was never aware of what it would take to acknowledge, accept, embrace and implement my findings. This part can be almost impossible if you are not willing to walk the talk. You might be thinking, come on Josephine, spill the beans, what do you mean, and how did you discover this entirely?

Well, even though I have shared my story a number of times and continue to embrace my inside-out healing that I share with others whom I support, my personal story still makes me feel emotional and sad and excited because I know the impact it creates for those in a similar situation. It inspires them to have the courage and build the resilience to get back up stronger than ever before by pointing them out and empowering them to reach out for person-centered help at all levels of their lives that will elevate them beyond their wildest imaginations.

YOU DO NOT HAVE to be a victim forever. You get to choose. There will always be triggers in your life but if you get equipped with the tools you need when need arises, Sunshine, this can be your go to resource either in your life or business, because you are not allowing the difficult times to become your destiny.

When you embody this, your productivity, positive attitude to almost everything will be infectious and your energy will enable you to attract those people you are looking to serve while standing out from the crowd.

Let me share with you how I came to where I am today.

It all started on Friday evening, 21 April 2017, when I was hit by a supermarket trolley. What happened was that I was trying to do some shopping across the dairy aisle when I heard this big bang behind me. I immediately felt like I was in another world, an illusion, but then realised that I had been knocked over with a fully loaded cage, also known as a supermarket trolley that is used to carry goods on or off the shelves. In the process, my right leg and foot were injured. I was in high heels, which led to me stumbling and twisting my right ankle inwards. It still saddens and breaks my heart every day to remember it. It's been over 5 years now, but I still struggle with the physical challenge of not being able to mobilize on my feet without the aid of a wheelchair.

I found myself in a situation I never imagined as my health continued to deteriorate. I took on all the advice from various professionals, friends, and family, but this did not make any improvement until I chose to take ownership of my life.

I had been through enough, and I had had enough. I knew no one else was experiencing exactly what was challenging in my life. I struggled to do the day to day tasks, my son at the age of 5 became a young caretaker, which was disorganising, frustrating, energy-draining and unexplainable. This was not what I had hoped for in life. I wanted to be the best mum and be able to create fun memories of his childhood, not traumatising memories.

THE DAY I realised that my son was now classified as a young caretaker was the same day I knew everything had to change. I had to do whatever it would take, despite any hurdles in my path. I had to think ahead, to find him help and seek help for myself as I was in a very big financial crisis that I had never wanted to think about or resolve. First, I was embarrassed by my circumstances, and secondly, I did not want to confront the option of being declared bankrupt. I knew that was the only way after my job contract was terminated, due to my absence after the injury.

In order for me to move forward, I was aware that it was not going to be easy. However, it was for a great cause, so worth it. Instead of feeling bad and sorry for myself, I started to practise mindfulness through bible study, prayer, and worship. That enabled me to gradually let go of what no longer served me. I allowed myself to unlearn what I once knew and was told to relearn getting back up again. This, I implemented every single day to carry on. I deserve better, and so do my loved ones, especially my son. That was my mantra.

I also remember a quote that I put beside my bed that said, "I am doing this for me, I am doing this to get better, and I am doing this for Jayden."

I had established that the medications had strong side effects that did not help unless I was sleeping. Waking up meant that I had to take more of the medicine. This is when the severe symptoms of depression, stress and anxiety began.

I did not want this to carry on longer than it had already been. I knew I was against some key professional people who had questions about my parenting skills, even though they knew I was struggling, so I was working to prove them all wrong. I had lost people I thought were close friends. It was a lonely place to be, but as a Christian believer, that was the cross for me to carry, even when I was scared and in fear. Courage, being strong and having a reason bigger than myself to do what I had to do was non-negotiable.

Somehow, I had to look towards the brighter side each time I wanted to give up. Even though my most immediate family was far, I managed to find authentic friends who I can now call my family. They held me accountable, believed in me, encouraged me, and advised me. I was inspired to actively work through what was keeping me stuck and playing small, because I knew I had so much to give and offer in the world which I did not want to die inside of me unshared or unheard.

In August of 2020, I published my first self-help book on Amazon, *The Revolutionary Breakthrough: How to turn your setback into a purposeful comeback.*

In 2020 I also collaborated with 23 amazing women, who were on a similar journey of unleashing their power through self-love and published a book called Love Thy Body, Vol 1. This went on to be a bestseller in late 2020.

In 2021, as I was evolving and keen to share what was happening in my personal life, an opportunity came and I was asked to collaborate with another group of ladies to publish a book called Seen, Vol 1. This was about sharing how I stepped into my purpose, passion and power which became a bestseller too. The most important and unique aspect of this collaboration was that we all agreed to share our proceedings from this book to go towards a charity organization that supports women with mental health challenges, which is a cause close to my heart.

My positive attitude towards actively working through adversity has been embraced by many who have provided incredible feedback to me. I have been featured in local and national and international press, blogs and radio sharing my story and creating awareness around how we women in the business of changing the world can achieve this.

In 2021 I was nominated and received an honorary award for women's empowerment (women appreciating women) and recently in 2022 I was nominated to receive an intellect award as a woman of vigour from Charles Waters Council/Society for Innovation & Research.

Best of all, my lessons, experiences and personal growth developments have enabled me to help other courageous women who want to be more and do more in life identify their potential and purpose not only after a personal injury but also, those who have experienced contemporary challenges of trauma and setbacks in their lifetime through my own unique signature program.

YOU MIGHT BE FEELING ALONE, but you do not have to go through tough times alone because you are not alone. To get the best outcome when working on becoming the best version of yourself, you do not have to pretend that everything is okay if it isn't. This is step one of my self-care routine. I identified my self-worth, which boosted my self-confidence without comparing myself to others or feeling any less than anyone due to my physical and mental health challenges. I knew I was enough, no matter what. l now love and accept who I am, and so can you.

Now that I've learned how to process all that I have experienced and am still experiencing, even with ongoing challenges such as a diagnosis of Functional Neurological Disorder (FND) with symptoms of Complex Regional Pain Syndrome (CRPS), which affects me every single day in the form of chronic pain, my days are not the same.

I have bad days, but also not-so-bad days. However, I have found a way of stepping into my passion and purpose of helping others on similar journeys so that they, too, can have the freedom to create a life of love that lifts them up. That is what I aim for while being supported by my wheelchair to get to places that I would have never been if I did not accept this aid. This has enabled me to unlock a lot of opportunities I never thought possible, to work and collaborate with some of the most amazing humans in the world, due to my tenacity, resilience and sharing my story to show others that they can do the same.

I now feel so blessed that my son is in a much better place and we both have a wonderful support system that works effortlessly to ensure that we do not backslide. This is what you want in your personal life in order to not only transform your life but also the lives of those many women in the world who are looking to you to share your own brilliance and how you can be a hero for them through your personal journey.

I am inviting you into a place of being in control of yourself, taking your power back into your hands. If you are still feeling scared or unsure, know that this is a great thing because you are about to have your breakthrough of stepping into your own greatness. You feel afraid because having a breakthrough means a lot to you. You are scared because you care.

Take the leap of faith, understand that to get through your personal challenges, those you have been able to speak about and yet to, you should be willing to do something that you have never done before. You can do this!

If you feel you would like to explore yourself more, I would like you to connect with me using my linktree details in my author's bio, as I do have some special offers for you that you may benefit from depending on where you are in your life or business.

Remember that if you can look up, you can definitely get up. Do not try to do it all by yourself, doubt yourself, or talk yourself out of what could transform your life through those you are here to serve.

In conclusion, I have realized that life experience, be it through chronic pain, childhood trauma, setbacks in your relationships, business, or health, cannot define you if you do not allow it.

I have learned that you can definitely get through anything that life has thrown at you by identifying improved alternative ways tailored to your personal capability if you are willing to go an extra mile to actively work through what seems to be challenging in your life. Know that you have got the key to your happiness, joy, freedom and success when you decide to rise above your personal challenges.

JOSEPHINE S N KALAGIRA

Josephine Sandra Kalagira is a best-selling Author, global speaker and the visibility and brand story mentor. Helping entrepreneurs to own and communicate their personal story with confidence so they can boost their visibility, expand their reach and impact effortlessly and grow an engaged audience using my unique signature program.

linktr.ee/JosephineSandraKalagira

THE TREK TO HELPING OTHERS AND CHANGING THE WORLD

BY RENA MCDONALD

Growing up, I always had plans. I knew what I wanted, and I always made it happen.

It did not occur to me until much later that some of the things I accomplished were remarkable. I was the first woman in my family to attend college and the only person to ever get a doctoral degree. I started a business at a relatively young age, and I did it all without a safety net or thoughts of not accomplishing it.

I KNEW things would be hard, and they were. But I never focused on those things, as I always viewed them as another hurdle to jump or mountain to climb to reach my goal.

It wasn't until after I became an attorney that I can recall being told I couldn't do something. The legal industry was primarily male dominated with many alpha personalities. I had been around strong men my whole life, but it never occurred to me that I wasn't an equal. I never took it seriously, or figured they must have meant someone else. It was the first time in my life that these jibes and jokes really started affecting me.

As a professional who had fought through undergrad and law

school, often working two jobs to pay for my tuition, I was shocked when I wasn't treated as an equal. In law school, you learn all about the rules and laws that fight discrimination and promote justice, so it was shocking that the very field that fought for other people's rights often was the biggest perpetrator of sexism and bigotry.

Oh "Sweetie"

I WAS OFTEN REFERRED to as "Sweetie" and "Honey" in boardrooms or Court room hallways. My ideas and arguments were often disregarded, or taken by someone else and promoted as theirs.

I recall an incident where I worked on a brief for many days with little sleep and after proudly handing it over to my superior, he called me an idiot because there was one grammatical error on page 19 of the 150-page document. He then proceeded to throw the whole thing in my face and laugh at me. I wondered if something had been wrong with me my whole life, but that no one had ever mentioned it. Maybe I had only gotten into law school as a joke or a prank. I began to believe that I wasn't smart enough to be an attorney.

Perhaps it was just that I listened to those voices for the first time, but I was heavily impacted, for the first time in my life, with self-doubt.

Despite that, I knew I wanted to be an attorney to help people and I knew that I could do better than the firms I was working with.

Big Changes in Little Packages

I opened my law firm at the start of the Great Recession and almost immediately got pregnant with my first son.

Unfortunately, rather than enjoy this time, I began to experience overwhelming anxiety. Perhaps it was being a mother that made the negative voices so much louder. Regardless, for the first time, I began to believe that I couldn't do anything, and that I wasn't all that I thought I could be.

I look back at the way my male counterparts would laugh when I told them I had opened my own practice. They "offered" to take my calls when it didn't work out and I needed a job.

My pregnancy with my son was very complicated and required extensive medical treatment. While the financial costs were high, they did not compare to the stress and anxiety of worrying about my son's health.

I DID REALIZE, however, how incredibly fortunate I was to be working for myself at that time. For the last three months of the pregnancy, I had at least 2 medical appointments a week. I recognized that I would never have been able to take care of my son that way had I been working for someone else.

I came to realize that owning my own business could be extremely beneficial for my family. And somewhere, that old inner voice that knew I could do anything started speaking again. I just had to really listen for it. I now had a family counting on me, and after looking at my son for the first time, I refused to fail.

I assumed that nothing would change with my clients after I gave birth. I was wrong. I lost serval clients because they felt I couldn't be as focused on their matter now that I had a child. I have a friend that also had a son around the same time. We graduated together and were at similar places in our legal careers. We met to congratulate each other on our new births. It was shocking that as the father of his son, not only was he not suffering from the lack of sleep frustrations, but his clients also had done nothing more than congratulate him on being a dad. The difference in our experiences was shocking.

Balancing Act

I have grown to hate the word balance, specifically as it applies to work and life. It became the new code word for having it all and looking great on social media as you did it.

I silently began to resent the amazing social media posts of my friends and relationships. I didn't realize until years later when I ran into an old friend, and she made a comment about how she was embarrassed by herself because she saw me on social media and knew I was doing great that I had become that person. I told her it was all a lie and that I was a S^%$ show and we both had a laugh. But at the time, I struggled to hold myself out to everyone as a success.

The first few years of owning my own business were more about proving I could than actually doing.

Not only could I not figure out how to balance everything, I was too busy to even commit any time to thinking about it. What got attention was what was on fire at that moment. I could only focus on deadlines, crying babies, bills, etc. I had no planning because I never slowed down enough to know that I could plan anything.

I want to be clear that I don't resent these times. I was proving to myself again that I could be, or do, anything. I needed that time, my family needed that time, my business needed that time. I remember many huge successes that perhaps at the moment I didn't celebrate as I was immediately onto the next thing.

Within a year, I had my first office and first real employee. Within 2 years, I added a second employee and we had to grow to a bigger space. My beautiful son was healthy and strong, and we gave him a brother to play with.

Despite all the success, that word balance kept making me cringe and making me feel like I was not doing enough. It wasn't until after the birth of my second son when I was speaking at a networking event, that I realized something was wrong. Someone asked me about my hobbies or what I did for fun... I was completely stumped. Every thought that came to mind started with "I used to..."

I realized that I was not doing anything for me, and what's worse, I didn't even know what I would want to do.

Fun? Isn't Doing Everything Enough??

That question became another obstacle to overcome.

I started doing crafts and home projects that I had previously enjoyed. While they were fun, they weren't satisfying my need to do more. I don't mean that I needed more things to do. I was and am very busy. It was an internal need to have a goal, figure out what makes me happy, and lay a plan for getting it done.

I have never been very physical, but I had a friend who was going through a hard time that wanted to start running. I REALLY did not want to go, but she is amazing, and I wanted to do whatever I could to make things easier for her. We committed to our first half marathon 6 months later. Unfortunately, not long after, she was injured and had to take a break. But I had committed. It was on Facebook and I had to do it after I posted about it. Not really, but that's what I thought at the time. So, I continued training on my own.

You may ask yourself how I did that. Well, I got less sleep. I woke up very early and went running before 5 am, alone in the dark, so that I could be home by the time my kids were up and needed to go to school. I don't recommend this, and now know that it is OK to tell everyone that they have to get themselves ready so that you can sleep a bit longer. But at the time, I made it work.

WHAT'S important is that running gave me some space. At first, I spent it all thinking about my cases and what I needed to do next. Then I started thinking about my relationship with my husband and how I could work to improve it. Then I started thinking about my kids. Then I started thinking about my business. These all felt like huge puzzles that needed to be focused on and broken down.

I realize now that these were all excuses to avoid focusing on what really needed the work: me.

Eventually, I started thinking about where I was at (not physically, I usually took the same road so I didn't have to pay attention), why I felt that I needed to do more, and what I could do to get there.

I remembered the little girl who would watch the People's Court and know that I could help those people win their cases. I remembered that I could do anything, and couldn't understand why other people thought that was hard. I remembered why I wanted to be an attorney and what led me to my own business. It wasn't social media or having an image that I had become so focused on. I really truly like helping people. It gives me so much satisfaction and happiness. I legitimately want the world to be better for having been in it. Having those few minutes alone and really talking to myself helped me reconnect with who I was.

Why helping others is important

Meanwhile, the world was getting angrier.

Politics have become insane, in my opinion. I don't care which party you belong to, we have become so ugly with each other, it's now a show that doesn't get much done except spit hate and discontent. I realize that if I want to make a difference, I need to look around at the people in my community. To satisfy this need, I want to look into the eyes of the people I work for and really know it makes a difference.

I started thinking about issues that are important to me, that I care about. I was in a very abusive relationship as a young woman, a relationship that opened my eyes to the cruelty and abuse that makes up so much of some people's lives. As a mother, I feel an overwhelming need to protect children from the harsh reality of these situations, so I began volunteering with several organizations that helped abused women and their children.

I was invited to sit on the board of a local women's shelter. It was often thankless hard work. Despite that, I made an effort to connect with the children at every opportunity. Knowing that my efforts helped them in any way was such a privilege.

I also spoke of it often to my children, and got them involved as much as possible. Watching them flourish and appreciate their lives was amazing. I knew I could do more.

I am very active in my community and perhaps because of my early attempts to promote myself through social media I am known in my area. At the suggestion of a friend, I took some leadership classes and really learned to recognize the value of growing a team of employees for your business.

ULTIMATELY, these lessons led me to involve my business and my team in my philanthropic efforts. I have found this to be incredibly beneficial to my business and now work to convince other corporations to do the same. My firm chooses several organizations a year and we work on various projects to help those organizations. Since we initiated this as a company, we have flourished.

Community service is great for morale. All professional environments can be stressful, but I believe working in a law firm is incredibly challenging. Our clients are with us for, in some cases, years at a time. We become confidants to their biggest desires and fears. We help them during their darkest hours. We are responsible for making sure they get to keep their homes, fight for their stolen assets, open and close their businesses, or maintain relationships with their children. Working in this field can sometimes make you feel like other people's lives are at stake.

DOING something for others that need help in a way you can control is an amazing counterweight for a law firms' responsibilities. When you hand someone a meal, you know that they get to eat today and you were a small part of that. Performing community service as a firm allows us to help others and immediately receive the gratification that comes from that and it's a great morale booster.

Philanthropy is a great team-building exercise. I encourage everyone to find projects or community organizations that are important to them. Thus, they get to share their interests in a positive way with the rest of the team.

I also find the activities to really promote teamwork and kindness. Spending a few hours together in the cold wind handing out blankets really makes you appreciate your warm coffee at your desk. Experiencing that together helps them build positive relationships that blend into the office and teamwork there.

There is no doubt that Community service helps the community you live in to be a better place. Knowing that you can make a difference or help people find services to benefit them helps everyone. The community becomes healthier and more financially stable. I have had past clients who are aware of our efforts and reach out when they are in need. Also, that level of community pride is evident in my staff, who continue to work to help others. In this way I am sharing my need to help and making it a priority for my entire staff.

Another huge benefit of public service that many other business owners seem to overlook is networking. Some of my largest clients have come to us as a result of our activities. Additionally, you do get a lot of free public exposure through social media and advertising. Many studies have shown that being top of mind is a big factor when consumers are making choices about who they want to do business with. Having seen your name associated with something you care about gives you a boost.

As I sit here today, the interesting thing is that if you ask me how we do it, I would laugh and shrug and say if you want to, you just do it. It is about balance (that dreaded word), it's about believing in yourself, and it's about helping others. In the end, it's about being you and doing what makes you happy.

RENA MCDONALD

Rena McDonald is the managing partner of McDonald Law Group, a general civil litigation firm operating since 2007. Rena and her firm have been recognized for their achievements and have won many awards including Top 100 Lawyers, Best Business Firm in Henderson, Top 100 Women in Las Vegas and Top 15 Bankruptcy Firms. Rena has also been featured in several magazines and identified as a "person to know" in Southern Nevada.

Rena McDonald is committed to serving the Las Vegas community. Rena was born and raised in Las Vegas and is very involved in improving her community. Rena was also recognized by the Henderson Chamber of Commerce and other organizations for her community service efforts.

Rena is a best-selling author, entrepreneur, and mother.

REDEFINING CUSTOMER SERVICE
BY JUDY GRANLEE-GATES

There is a legendary tale from the mid-1970's about a guy in Alaska who took two tires into a Nordstrom Store and asked to return them. Now, we all know that Nordstrom hasn't and likely never will, sell tires, but they did indeed take the tires "back" and give the customer a refund, despite that they never sold them, and without a receipt.

The story was later confirmed by Blake Nordstrom, who commented publicly that the salesperson "used great judgment and treated the customer like he would want to be treated". The store location that took the return, had previously been a tire shop, and according to legend, the salesperson felt that it was the least he could do.

Finding my way

At age 12, in 1976, I began a long line of jobs that were heavy on customer service. I started my own small business in 1988, working in it to this day. I build and remodel homes, and providing a higher level of service than most builders and a quality product has always been my number one driver. It's a hard business to manage expectations in, so much is unseen, and must be imagined until it is built. It can be a challenge for those that are not able to visualize concepts that are not physically in front of them.

I have learned to carefully manage expectations, I have had customers burst into tears on a job site when they first saw something they chose as a finished product (thank goodness this is rare) and I have heard the words "I didn't think it would look like that" so many times, I need it tattooed somewhere. But over the decades, I have learned to clearly spell out our customer experience goals, and to manage things at each turn for the best experience.

The Truth *about Customer Service*

This brings us to that all-important question. Is the customer always right? I am going to be the one to say it out loud. The customer is not always right. *Gasp.* I said it! In print!

Even I, as a customer, am not always right. I'm guilty of "scanning" things and not fully reading, and I am disappointed on occasion for my lack of "due diligence". While I would like to blame someone else, I can't.

In building and remodeling, things can change very quickly. I had a customer, Lisa, who chose her appliances, and we placed a large deposit to order them. Months later, the cabinets came and were installed. Then I got the call. The appliance company had ordered all Lisa's appliances, and when they came in, Lisa's range had been sold to someone else, as a salesperson thought we could order another one "in time." Cue the pandemic, where nothing is as it should be. Scrambling to get a replacement, I found that we only had THREE ranges that were available in time to move Lisa in. All were more expensive; one was double the cost. Long story short, I ended up paying for half the cost of Lisa's range. My integrity was on the line here, and it was time for me to step up.

In the 1970's, when those tires were returned, the world was a simpler place. Research was done by encyclopedia or a trip to the library to talk to the research librarian. The internet wasn't even a concept, computers for personal use were just a dream two guys were tinkering with in a garage. Many stores did not even accept returns, you bought it and you owned it. Return policies like Nordstrom, became a way to differentiate your business from the competition, and it has been a hallmark for many companies. Customers did not have access to the information we do now, and they had to place their trust in the salespeople that were offering the goods as the "experts."

THE INTERNET CHANGED this drastically in the mid 1990's when it became a widely-used tool, with access to almost anything you could want to know. It changed how people got information, did research, and how people purchased things. Customers now had enough information to be not only knowledgeable, but also sometimes self-appointed experts.

They also got some bad information. When I'm at Home Depot and overhear the advice that some of the workers offer customers that have come in looking to fix a problem, I *cringe* at some of their suggestions.

As time went on, the internet archives became more robust, and literally nothing was sacred or not able to be found online. I think this shift gave people a sense of the curtain being pulled back, and a glimpse into whatever it was they might want to need to know. And now they know just enough to be dangerous.

Tony was a recent customer that was upset over pandemic delays. He was a businessperson as well, experiencing the same delays and shortages I was. When a part of his order was not available, and he had been told that repeatedly as part of managing expectations, his temper tightened as his project neared completion, and I received an unhappy email from Tony stating he felt the company should compensate him for the delay.

I HAD WARNED Tony of lead times and delivery issues, kept them updated weekly, made extra trips to his job to make sure install was going well, and offered help when there was some confusion. Had the tables been turned, I don't believe that Tony would have given me any discount, but he sure expected one from me for his "inconvenience" during a global pandemic and supply chain crisis.

THIS SCENARIO MIRRORS the spectrum of companies today trying to struggle with, balance, and succeed at customer service.

But let's back up. Does a store that never sold tires, ever, really get high marks for refunding a customer for something everyone on earth knows they don't carry? From a commonsense perspective, no, but I often hear people say, "That's why I shop at X, because they will take anything back." I see the value, but is it a realistic model for all businesses? Companies like Nordstrom have an annual revenue in the 15 billion range. Can they afford to take a tire back? Yes. But if they are a smaller company, with maybe 1 million in revenue, can they afford to do the same? Can they still provide great service even without taking tires back?

If I go to my hairdresser with a photo of a new style I want, and the model in the photo has curly hair and I have stick-straight hair, a smart hairdresser / businessperson will stop to manage my expectations by pointing out that my hair is straight, and not well suited for the cut. They may say, "We can do this cut, but it will require a perm or daily curling with an iron to get the look." They may let me know I might be dedicating a lot of time to styling my hair since I don't have that hair type. And, if they are wise, they will say no to the haircut and offer me another option better suited to my hair type and texture so that I can easily replicate the style at home and will be happy with my cut. If they don't do that, and just cut my hair, I am likely to be quite unhappy and walk around telling everyone just that.

Consider the challenges that some business types bring. Years ago, I did a large remodel for a lovely customer who had some old Moire taffeta wallpaper in her home. In its day it had been lovely, but the number one rule in remodeling is that "new shiny things make old crappy things look older and crappier." I say it all the time. The customer loved the wallpaper, and though faded and worn in spots, she felt that it would be a nice touch to all the new spaces. I discouraged keeping it and provided her with the cost to remove, which at that time was over $3,500, very labor-intensive to remove the paper with a steamer, scrape the walls, mask everything and retexture, then repaint. The customer felt that was too much money, and she was already at her budget.

The end of the remodel came, and we met on-site for her walk-through. The new work looked amazing, and I'll admit, the wallpaper was a disappointment all throughout the house. The customer walked in, and said to me, "it's so beautiful Judy, *but I wish you had MADE me take the wallpaper down."*

I CANNOT TELL you the disappointment I felt. *Made* you? I begged you! I reminded you with my snappy catch phase of how old crappy stuff looks worse when new stuff goes in. I did everything I could to make it easy to say yes to taking it out. The customer was right and got to choose.

In the end, she was disappointed over something only SHE had control over. To this day, 20 years later, I have recounted this story to every customer I work with. Some get to hear it multiple times. And to this day, it was the most disappointing customer experience I have had with a customer of mine. Zero control on my end, all the responsibility.

THE ENTITLED CONSUMER

In the last decade, we have seen the emergence of what many refer to as the "entitled consumer": customers who believe they are special and deserving of immediate attention and that a business should comply immediately with their needs. This is "the customer is right" pushed to the extreme.

The entitled consumer is the one who is flying through the air at 500 miles per hour on an airplane 30,000 miles above the earth with several hundred others, yet instead of being in awe of that modern miracle, they are annoyed that the Wi-Fi is too slow.

The entitled consumer makes up over 75% of all consumers by some reports, and these are the people that expect more than is ever reasonable. Like the guy who returned the tires.

RE-DEFINING *Customer Service for your Business*

So how do we manage our customers' experiences, balance that with our own businesses, and keep everyone happy? Do we take back items we don't sell, or give profit away because an item was late? Do we say yes to anything they ask so they won't go on the internet and say terrible things about us?

Customer service is not about refunds. It is about the experience, start to finish. It's more about the peaks, and not nearly as much about the valleys.

Buying a bottle of shampoo is a very different buying experience than building a home. Dining out at a restaurant is a different experience than purchasing a car. Successful businesses recognize that customer experiences vary, but that great companies have clearly defined goals about their customer experience, and they make that available to their customers.

Do you have things that truly are out of control if you are the customer? In some industries, the customer is not always right, because there is a higher power that IS the final word. Building code, for example, dictates what I can and can't do within a structure. A customer may want something that is not allowed by code, and if we proceed, the job will be stopped by a building official until corrected. There can be workarounds, but in some cases, the customer may not like any of them, but that doesn't mean they get to do it anyway.

Each customer service "issue" is an opportunity to learn, improve and do better. I strive to have a highly satisfied customer, but even I have to admit, I do not have a 100% track record.

Mike and Linda came to me for a major remodel, with completed plans from their architect. At framing, we found the plans were not accurate, and were not able to be built in the way shown. Many builders would have stopped and said, "Call us when your architect fixes this." But I don't bring my customers problems, I bring them solutions.

I called my favorite plan designer, and we created a new layout, fixed the issues, and THEN I went to Mike and Linda. I explained the issues and presented the fix. They saw the problems clearly and were relieved that I had come to them with a solution.

CREATING *a Great Customer Experience*

How do you create the customer experience for the folks that you deal with daily? First, we look at what we think is important to the customer to make the experience a great one.

HOW DO we want the customer to feel during the process and after? What can we offer that others can't or don't? Communication, integrity, educating, examples of quality workmanship for intangibles are all ways we can help to provide a great customer experience.

I had a wonderful facial at a local resort. My esthetician wrote down detailed notes of things she wanted me to do at home, and she made me sample jars of several products to try. Her time spent giving me these tips in writing and samples were out of the norm in my experience, and they helped me resolve some skin care issues I was unhappy with. She earned my loyalty and repeat business from this simple yet thoughtful act.

IN MY COMPANY, we strive to have our clients' experience be one that is educational, interactive and fun. I once built for a friend, and she said to me "you don't do all this stuff for every client, do you?" when I provided paint samples and design boards for her to choose from. Yes, I do! It's what sets us apart.

One way we can build our own customer service program is by doing a core values exercise. It's easy, and it helps create guideposts and measuring tools when issues arise, we can look to our core values to guide us in the heat of the moment.

Start by making a list of values by asking the question "What is important at our company and what makes working here unique?" This list might include words like transparency, honesty, autonomy, independence, fun, accountability, passion, teamwork, trust, and more. Your list should be 10-15 words long.

Next, write each word on a small square of paper, lay them all out on the table. Identify the very most important one, the one that speaks loudest to you, and place it near the top of the table. Repeat the exercise until you have narrowed it down to 5 to 7 core values. Record and print these out, these are your company's guiding principles.

IN MY COMPANY, they are integrity, problem solving, innovation, value, and continuous improvement.

Use statements to define each value. Then build your mission statement around your core values.

HOW DO core values help me create a customer service plan? When I encounter a problem, I can compare it to my core values. There have been times in my career where something was overlooked or missed, like something we had verbally agreed on that did not make it into the contract. Without that item in the contract, it could be very easy to say, "That is not part of the scope of work" and move on, or bill the customer for the change. But one of my core values is integrity, and part of our mission statement says, "Our spoken word is better than anything we could ever put in writing."

When I look to my core values, the answer is clear: I need to honor my word.

Striving for Excellence

By defining our company's core values, we can be unique, authentic, and create an excellent environment for our ideal customers, attracting people who are aligned towards our values and experiences. When we align our values with our customer service, we stand out and we make it easier to attract the "right" customers to our business. When we attract the right customers, it is much easier to manage the experience.

IT TAKES a brave soul to be a small businessperson, and it feels vulnerable to set your values out on display. But take pride in the values and let them guide you in all you do. Your customers will benefit, and rave about both your product and process.

WHILE WE CAN'T MANAGE everything, and we can't prevent all scenarios, we can do the work up front to set our own policies, expectations, and procedures. We can make them known to the customer, and we can seek agreement that this will be how we operate should we engage in business together. In the end, the customer may not be right, but they can *still* have an excellent experience regardless.

JUDY GRANLEE-GATES

A fourth-generation small business owner, Judy Granlee-Gates has worked in customer service jobs for 46 years, (including a brief stint at Nordstrom) and strives for continual improvement in her processes. She is a driven problem solver and uses that skill to benefit her customer's experience. An award-winning custom home builder and remodeler, dozens of her projects have been recognized on local, state and national levels and her company received a Pacesetter Award from Custom Home Magazine for outstanding customer experience. Judy utilizes her degree in Education, Training and Development to take her customers through the homebuilding and remodeling process with confidence, fun and outstanding results.

She loves defying the odds of construction projects being stressful and traumatic, and delights in helping clients have fun and enjoy the process as well as the result.
    linktr.ee/judygranleegates

A MARKETING LOVE STORY: IDEAS TO CHANGE THE GAME
BY DANNIE CADAVID

"Our world needs more conscious people and businesses. How are you planning to impact the world?"

This was the final statement of my first-ever intervention in public, before officially becoming a Brand Consultant at The Ideas Factory.[1]

The year was 2015, the audience predominantly male, the subject: "Build your brand strategy for sustain growth."

It was an epic fail.

In the eyes of the audience, I was young and too romantic. Why would I ask them to think about value & impact when all they needed were some quick hacks for the recently baptized field of digital marketing? I embarrassed myself.

A HEART WAS BROKEN

The thing is, I planned that workshop with some contradictory ideas fighting in my brain. That was the year when thousands of

Syrian refugees desperately migrated to Europe, only to find death and rejection; yet people were still deciding if the dress was golden or blue?

I'M SORRY MARKETING, but I don't believe in you!

My strong sense of justice and a lack of faith in humanity were fighting against the years of marketing training and the buzzwords of the digital world. In the middle of this, a heartbroken Me was seeing how my values and my profession were completely misaligned.

Then, an idea struck: What if I start teaching business owners to connect their economic benefit with a sense of purpose? I could create a humanized and conscious approach to marketing! I felt so proud of myself.

OUR WORLD NEEDS MORE conscious people and businesses. How are you planning to impact the world?

Now you know how it all went that day.

A SAD BALLAD and a lucky encounter

I changed careers a few days after that presentation. Found a space in one of my dad's social projects, went back to study Physics and got a gig at a local bar to support my "in-between."

I didn't think about marketing for months. Nothing improved in my life. It turned out I missed marketing, at least the part where I could tell stories that tap into people's emotions. *To me, marketing is all about love, joy, nostalgia and excitement.*

At risk of sounding like a sad ballad, I crawled back to marketing. At that moment, it was more of a financial decision. But faith knows how to play its game, because that trivial step led me to the greatest journey of my life.

In 2016, a less romantic me met Jes Schroeder, a force of nature.

Shamelessly following her heart, without a hint of Spanish, or limitations. Just a country girl trying to make sense of the world, and someone who always knew that the world was bigger than her Australian landscapes. Always in motion, restless and with an unconditional faith in humanity that could only be paired with my lack of social skills.

I didn't realize back then, but Jes's unique ability to energize the best in each person, awakened my love and dream of *creating a new version of marketing.*

A LOVE WAS BORN

Not all love stories start the same. Not all love stories are about two people. Not all love stories are a stereotype.

Between the Spanglish, the long-working hours and empty wine bottles, *The Ideas Factory (TIF)* came to life, after realizing two simple things.

First, for some mysterious reason, sometimes the days do have more than 24 hours, especially when you are as obsessed with quality as we are.

Second, that there was something immaterial whose strength and value could be measured only by its degree of madness, something rare and, because of it, invaluable: *we discovered the value of an idea and the power of collaboration between opposing points of view to create unexpected results.*

Starting as a way to infuse companies with creative ideas, TIF began to show traces of the transforming force that carried within, moving from a short campaign to becoming a business leader's advice source, due to our own questioning attitude and an addiction to challenges.

THROUGHOUT THIS JOURNEY, we have resized and reshaped, learned and unlearned, agreed and disagreed, to become the meaningful and conscious version we are today: *A strategic & creative agency dedicated to shape purposeful brands to make a positive impact in the world. A creative force for good!*

Challenge **the norm**

I see our roles in marketing and advertising as a great responsibility.

The need to sell, and the ability of marketing professionals to influence people's behavior has shaped the world for hundreds of years. Today, we are living in the result:

- Destructive consumption habits affecting health, emotional wellbeing and the environment
- Unhealthy beauty concepts
- Gender stereotypes
- Group identity replacing self awareness
- Culture of impatience and instant rewards
- Self-centered brands & self-centered online content
- Materialism above personal growth
- And, my new personal favorite, green washing and the world of empty promises

All of this, old and new, set the current dynamics of our society.

But if, with one single decision on our business model, piece of advertising, or product attributes, we were powerful enough to create all those problems, we should be equally able to re-shape the world into a more sustainable, respectful and fair version.

That's precisely what we aim to do everyday through our **Purpose-led branding & purpose-led marketing.**

An act **of insurrection to the typical "win now, fix later" of our digital era**

Crafted upon the concept of **value creation**, from the story, identity and communication assets, all the way up to the business model and philanthropy factor of a company or brand, this science-based process is founded in the following concepts:

1. **Put strategy back to Branding:** A brand is not a logo. It is a perception that lives on people's minds. A Brand Strategy is the conscious process of defining what that perception could and should look like. It encompasses the learning and finding of the purpose and difference, the articulation of both into structure, form, and format, as well as the integration with a marketing & business model to ensure the economic benefit and the possibility of creating a positive impact.
2. **Integrate sales process with value generation:** At the center of every need in marketing and communication are the sales results. In purpose-led marketing, the process goes from understanding a customer's actual needs to developing the right type of solution and adding value to their lives. The sale is just a natural consequence of that pairing. That is a difference you can create, tell, and deliver.
3. **Helping people vs selling to people:** Learning how the mind works and how to influence behavior shouldn't be used just to increase consumption. Understanding the socio-cultural and psychological context of an audience could help us identify potentially dangerous paradigms to develop the right type of communication to transform them into more positive dynamics.
4. **Redefining the competitive landscape:** We need to stop comparisons. We no longer compete. Instead, each brand and company works within the market group (tribe) most suited to who they are and what they represent. The only true value is on building relationships. The difference is in the way we connect and make our clients feel. The key is on building empathy.
5. **Avoid the aspirationalism of expectations:** As in love, in

marketing and brand communication, we have also hurt ourselves by setting expectations in the minds of users that can only lead us down the path of a poor product experience. It is always better to surprise, establishing realistic measures, delivering honesty and differentiating ourselves through a story that connects with their own history and sense of identity.
6. **Always expand the impact for the long term:** Highlight the social impact and commitment of each brand in the world.
7. **Make it sustainable in the short term:** Understand that financial resources are necessary even for supporting a greater cause. Develop smart tactical plans to allow the economic benefit in the short term and ensure growth.
8. **Make it tangible through business structure:** The results of marketing efforts depend more on the business model than on the right selection of tactics and channels. This is the step most business owners forget in the heat of the short term focus.

WE LOVE MAKING things fun and easy, so we sum it up with 5 simple pillars:

The rules of purpose-led marketing

1. Act like you give a damn!
2. Look beyond the obvious
3. Replace competition for collaboration
4. Prioritize ethics and actions with purpose
5. Unleash the crazy: break the tradition, be unapologetic, keep it real.

I WOULD LOVE to see in two generations from now how our small revolution has impacted people like us. I would love to see a world of purposeful brands.

IDEAS TO CHANGE **the game**

Since that iconic first presentation, I learned not only how to love marketing, but how to put love into marketing.

After seven years, I'm ready to ask again:

OUR WORLD NEEDS MORE conscious people and businesses. How are you planning to impact the world?

From my side, I'm dedicated to nurturing, guiding and supporting purposeful brands to become meaningful and successful. And, in the process, I'm co-creating with the next generation of marketing professionals to make sure this love story continues for many more iterations.

Are you in the process of building your own purposeful brand? Jes & I would love to hear your story. Let's have a cuppa!

DANNIE CADAVID

Dannie Cadavid is the Co-founder and senior Brand Strategist at The Ideas Factory Marketing Agency. Developing a game-changing mindset towards a more human, conscious and respectful approach to marketing, sales & advertising. She truly believes that brands have the ultimate power to shape and reshape the world, and that business can be run with an ethical, humanized approach and still be profitable. In the past six years Dannie and her group of brand professionals have worked with over 30 business leaders across the globe to transform their companies into purposeful and competitive brands.

Visit: theideasfactory.com.co/lets-have-a-cuppa

linktr.ee/dannie.cadavid

GRIT
BY POET KHAN RASS FIYAA

She looked right into my eyes.
Theresa Mendoza is my newfound hero. To watch her rise, reign, murder the game with brains and a fitted black dress, Glock to match. The representation received, witnessing a woman run an organization from the ground up. She was delicate, bold and most of all determined to overcome poverty.

Season five of the Queen of the South literally saved my life. It was not only the grand finale of an absolutely riveting series, The Queen Pin at the end/top with her friends/family, her love, and most importantly, with her planned and thought through success/wealth was affirming.

I realized that no excuse is worth the best parts of your life. Nothing is worth now, or the opportunity to make the life you want with the resources at hand.

As a mother, my reason to soar is also my deterrent at times. Learning to conquer the resistance of being fearless, allowing myself to dream big again.

Spark:

*When I was younger,
my dreams filled the corners of the sky.
I knew I could do anything with God on my side.*

I look at my kids and I realize that the parts of me where I feel insufficient, becoming a pandemic teacher, a mom, are the parts of me that are most valuable, and I am pretty damn good at teaching! The best thing is, giving myself the opportunity has shown me that I enjoy it as well.

*Success is subjective.
It boomerangs how you feel about yourself.
What do you feel you deserve in this life?
I like to point out facts, twirl them between my fingers like
    batons. I am learning to shine more emphasis on the
    abundance that is present, radiating, seeking
    engagement.*

I sulk over the lack of family, no reunions to attend, and then I think about Theresa. She lost it all at such a young age, no protection. She grew up on the streets of Culiacan, Mexico, parents' blood on her Sunday dress, in the grit, she formed her family. Pote, a friend she made along the way, became family that blood could not afford. Every obstacle, disabled with full consideration of who and where she was placed in this life, believing she deserved riches, and unapologetically focused.

People always say you must be clear with what you want: if you tell the universe you want "something" it'll bring you some thing; if you say you want a little, you will receive less than. Theresa demanded riches and her story aided in capping every excuse in my book. For that, I am profoundly obliged and will dedicate this chapter to the will of Theresa Mendoza.

What's the price of success? The decision to be successful.

Spirit:

Not by might
not by power, nor by hour
but, by spirit God, can you hear it?
Calling for ears that face fears, create canvases of contrast
My will will outwill the clay house washed away by mudslide
my soul must continue to seek the fountain, the frontier, innovator
my essence will pursue without ceasing a thirst for more knowings, blissful experiences.
My spirit, so loud you can hear it in everything I do
cosmic energy sprinkled strategically throughout my body,
I cry but I survive
I realize there are diamonds in these fountains
Mountains stretching so high they cast shadows that blanket traveled traumas.
let your river be exceedingly, stretched abundantly
May the ground beneath you be more than your support, foundation.
The Haitians, Ukraine, black America's pain, it's all the same
how the nation be so proud, loud about the business of gentrifying culture,
Docile that vigorous spirit, they say.
the passion be so loud, oh so proud
they can hear it
they can hear it
they can hear it and they do not want to,
do you?

I ENCOURAGE you to write your story.

> Attempt to comprehend,
> that the full expression of love
> desires you as its canvas,

and yes, full self-expression does involve the financial means.

I have been trying to get back into the workforce since January. I stayed home with my kids during COVID. I wrote 2 poetry books within that time, privileged to be included in several anthologies. It was a blessing in that way.

My oldest son was behind in school pre-COVID, and when we switched to virtual, things went from complete disengagement to me watching him trying to contain his temper, frustrated, crying. In honest reflection, for the last two years, I believed I lacked the ability to teach them, to take them from one place of knowledge and learn them to the next. My now 7-year-old has been home with us as well, home at this critical moment of learning how to read. I genuinely did not believe I could take them on a journey of expanding their minds, elevating them from one place to the next level. My efforts were futile.

Knowing I was wasting precious time was an elephant on my chest. I just was not ready.

SEVERAL ELEMENTS WERE instrumental in finding the courage to tackle the assignment of teaching my kids. Number 1, I had to realize that I have been teaching them all along and how could the "wordsmith" not be good at teaching words?

You see, teachers hold a special position next to the divine, they take on the responsibility of the next generation, not everyone is worthy of that responsibility.

Two weeks after watching season 5 of Queen of The South, I decided to take a trip to Los Angeles, CA. The first thing people say about California is that it is excessively expensive. However, when you arrive you witness it's not lacking in population. Sunsets were made in California. She's like me, no introduction necessary, you just know you have arrived at one of the most gorgeous places on earth. I intend to move back, that is how much of an impact it had on me. I would gladly work 8-hour days, five days a week with four side hustles to live in a place where I can have an abortion if I want to, where I can smoke cannabis without being afraid and/or feeling worthless, and, most importantly, have the ocean and the mountains in the same theatre.

California took all my vacation budget, a few days prior I told my boys, "Hey guys, I don't think this is a good idea, we shouldn't go," both of my sons replied, "Mom, let's go, let's go buy some luggage!" I decided in that moment to live, to take me and my 11-year-old and seven-year-old on a road trip to Los Angeles, CA, alone. I gave myself the best of everything that week, a 2021 Jeep Cherokee fully loaded, the Embassy Suites Premium floor in LAX, warm and easy to digest oatmeal and bottomless Jacuzzis. I did not deny myself one pleasure, not one, and it felt so good for money to not be an issue.

Abraham Hicks says, "We have to fake it till we make it." For seven days I pretended that I was the successful writer I aim to be. I loved myself. I strutted a two-piece down the Santa Monica beach shore, rubbed my belly, allowed my cellulit (yes lit) thighs to shine. My boys looked boundless, groomed and kept. We ate the best food, I drank nothing but top-shelf, attracted the best in the crowd, and literally met the most amazing people. It was exhilarating.

Two weeks prior to this, I was considering suicide. I hated myself, said I would count the pieces of peace once employment was established.

I was in a car wreck in 2018 which left me with an injured pinky toe. I was crippled for three years, resulting in my neck making crunching sounds when I turn it certain ways. In December of 2021, I had toe surgery. No longer crippled, I cannot do what I used to do, period. I have to be able to acknowledge my body's needs when necessary, sit down or stand up when I need to, and I realize the workforce does not idolize self-actualization.

I could not figure out my life, how to maintain my bills and the balance of being here for my boys and maybe an hour or two for myself a week. At that point, even poetry became offensive, "poeting" for monetary gain. I am a professional poet; I missed the freedom of doing it for fun.

Since returning to Texas, I have endeavored to keep this same vibration of luxury and abundance after submerging myself in a week of splurging. I was scarcely able to identify what abundance felt like until I "pretended" for an entire week, in a new location. I showed up as Poet Khan Rass Fiyaa and was received as such.

I SAID ALL that to say: take the ******* vacation. Plan it, so you can get all of what you deserve and dive headfirst. If someone wants to help you get where you're trying to go, allow them, allow the universe's guidance to experience abundance. You deserve it.

Prior to the trip, I was experiencing pains in my chest, trying to figure out how I was going to work, be at home, and still have time to pursue my dreams.

I lost all forms of predictable income in February: the child tax credit, the Uber eats job. Poetry and donations have sustained me. I had to affirm that my gift is indeed making a way for me, and that is true abundance.

My worth is not determined by having employment or the lack thereof. A job, no matter the statue, does not signify the quality of person I am. Lacking employment does not make me a bad mother, an unproductive citizen.

I also had to learn that when there is no way, you make a way, and from that dwelling came the idea of going into business for myself. I started Poems and Plates, Something for the Belly, Something for the Soul. I had to look around at the resources readily available to me and see what I could do with them. I love to cook healthy meals, and why not deliver a healthy plate with a poem of encouragement and affirmation? So, my kids and I did a test run, and it went well.

I had no business plan. It honestly came out of need, but people were receptive. Since then, I have invested in an LLC for myself, and am now scheming over life insurance policies, something I never saw myself doing.

I am so completely proud of myself. At my lowest point, I reached for me. We always think it's going to be something or someone outside of us, we always say: when I get this, when I achieve that, then I'll allot myself happiness.

If you know anything about the law of attraction, if you practice lack, lack will be your experience. Honestly? I rage at this part of the equation because how do you have something you've never had? How do you have luxury when all you know is poverty? You take a vacation and for four days you pretend that you are the number one read on Oprah's book club list. You get away from your current situation, 12 hours away, and pretend for 96 hrs that you are who you want to be.

I understand that something this drastic may not be financially feasible, but sometimes it is, and we just feel unworthy. Allow all the pleasure, "feel good" because the "feeling good" attracts more to feel good about in your life. I know what it's like to look around and have no reason to smile. That's when you must make a reset in your segment.

If you have been looking for a sign to take that vacation, to do something excessively expensive on every level just for your selfish pleasure, this is it. Shake up the energy in your atmosphere and then come back to your current situation with a plan. Plan to be the greatest you ever!

OPEN MY GIVING:

> *She craves voluntary shade on sunny days*
> *a paved way to gladness*
> *reinstated my CMA*
> *money conquers sadness so I conjure a way to conquer an*
>   *obscure route in pursuit of*
> *4 centuries worth of Loot, this one's for my roots*

I want a book release on a retreat
a slab of boss ladies eating cherries, rubbing each other's feet
renting out suites for the times we meet
me spitting poetry,
I want to be the CEO of me
filet mignon medium rare, chicken wings for my pair
The days I did not want to live are my sure found reason to give
I want to live
God, open my giving
I want to give so I can start living.
Everything I do is up to you
everything I do is up to you
I am blessed with the ability to forgive
I am ready to live.

POET KHAN RASS FIYAA

Born in the Gulf of Mexico, now residing in the El Paso Texas desert, a mother of two Suns.

A voice for prison reform, mental health, as well as Sensual Pleasure Poet pursuing her first dream of creating unconquerable spaces for vulnerability and sensuality in the poetic world. A King Maker, Queen mentor, A co-host of the award winning El Paso Barb Wire Open Mic Series which airs every Monday on Youtube. Published author of "CPR to My Dreams (An Ode to 2020)" which captures her experience with the onset of covid and rioting through her pen, & "My Abyss"(I wrote him free), a poetic depiction of incarcerated love. She has works included in 15 anthologies including "Salute to Black Women," "Once Upon A poem," & "Life In The Times," a Border Senses project in response to living in a pandemic. Her most recent publication is a chapter contribution to an anthology called "Feisty" which is a #1 seller on Amazon. Also a member of the Women's

Poetry Network "Tesoro." She is the CEO of Poet Khan Rass Fiyaa LLC offering services from editing, Khanpassion Yoga, and Poems n' Plates serving digestive friendly dishes. She is Love, Peace, Light and abundance.

linktr.ee/Poetkhan

BREAKING THE PATTERN OF EMOTIONAL ADDICTION

BY DESTINY DEHAVEN

I tried so many modalities, went to many seminars and personal development retreats. No matter what, I always was and continue to be *a Pattern Breaker*.

I have been doing this since I was a child. It is a part of my human design, and I'm phenomenal at it.

Through my own experiences I relate to other entrepreneurs and show them what they can have and how easy it can be. Life doesn't have to be hard. Owning and running a business doesn't need to be a struggle.

You can have what you want...when you want it...how you want it...and enjoy every minute of it.

This is the intention I will hold for you.

The Break Down

What's up SPARK reader and world-changer? It's your girl Destiny here, and *we've got a problem*.

But first, there are a few things I want you to know about my chapter before we continue:

1. We're going to dip our toe into the "woo," but I promise not to push you farther than you're willing to go.
2. I'm talking about addiction. But not the addiction you're used to.
3. We're told addiction is insurmountable and we need to hit rock bottom first. I don't believe this is true.
4. I absolutely love and adore my parents. They are amazing and did the best parenting they knew how to do. I do not blame them, nor hold them responsible for my addiction. Neither should you.

Back to the problem I mentioned. We have an addiction, and it's not to sex/porn, alcohol, smoking, or drugs of any kind. It's an addiction to an emotion.

We must break the pattern of our emotional addiction, because I believe in a world where patterns are meant to be broken.

3 years ago, I was sitting in a seminar room. The facilitator was talking about energy and how we can create it and make things happen. We can have what we want, do what we want, create EVERYTHING that we want, at the snap of our fingers.

Now, I know this is on the woo-woo side, and I admit it left me scratching my head. However, stick with me because it's going to make sense soon.

The facilitator then continued, explaining that you will create an emotion as well, since emotions are energy in motion.

But then she said the clincher, the piece that shook me to my core. She said: you'll create the emotion that you know, the one you experienced the most as a child. The emotion you are addicted to.

I felt all the breath in my lungs leave.

"Fuck!"

I sat back in my chair. I felt a visceral reaction and I knew.

I was addicted to anger and frustration. Although, there's a list of emotions that we can be addicted to: sadness, anxiety, overwhelm... I chose anger and frustration.

You see, as a child I knew two things to be true. First: if I cried, I better have a reason to cry, or else I would be given a reason. Second: if I was too excited or proud then that meant I was bragging, and I'd be knocked off my pedestal. Usually with a backhand or a metal stick, or a guava tree branch.

This meant being sad wasn't safe, and being happy or excited wasn't either.

After looking around at the adults in my life, I realized anger was the way to go.

No one bothered me when I was angry. No one backhanded me into a wall when I was angry. No one yelled or screamed at me when I was angry. As a matter of fact, they left me alone in my room, to read a book, play video games, or read Archie comics.

Anger was safe.

Anger was protection.

Anger left me untouched and unscathed. Well, on the outside at least.

Internally, there was so much more going on. When I was in high school, the yearbook teacher screeched at me because we had given every senior a quote, whether they picked one or not. Two students' parents pitched a fit about the quotes we chose. They weren't awful quotes, or awful students, but the parents were threatening to sue the school and the yearbook program.

Seething, I went for a walk. Why? The teacher signed off on the quotes and gave us permission to do this. Yet somehow it was my fault, and I was going to have to speak to the principal as well as the parents. The yearbook teacher yelled after me to come back into the room, I turned to glare at her and she retreated into the classroom.

While walking, my mind flooded with thoughts like: "But SHE said we could do it." "Ugh, you're in so much trouble." "Quit acting like a baby." "You're weak." "You knew this would happen," or "See, you deserve to be expelled." These thoughts were quickly followed by: "You're not worthy. You're useless." "You're a horrible person."

Ultimately, the anger overtook me. Exhausted by the rage and crying because it "wasn't fair," and I was "alone."

Sitting back in that seminar room, something clicked.

This awareness that I had to our addiction to emotions shifted how I work with my clients today. I realized this addiction was the missing piece to my stressed-out, overwhelmed, and scared clients and their breaking through to stop playing small, show up fully onstage, and make more money.

My awareness around emotional addiction made me a better coach and energy healer. It also made everything I had done in life make sense.

The Breakthrough

The energy we are addicted to stems from our childhood. No matter how good of a childhood you had, you experienced trauma. And let's not get into comparing our traumas…that's another Ted talk.

Back to our childhood trauma. Maybe as a kid we felt like we were abandoned, like no one was there for us. Our parents may have been in the room or sitting next to us, yet they may not have been paying attention and somehow, we translated that in our little minds as abandonment.

Maybe we were bullied as a kid…or maybe we were the bully. Maybe we stuffed our anger down time and time again only to have it explode at the least opportune time.

Each traumatic experience is tied to an energy that is linked to an emotion, such as: fear, rage, or sadness. If you pictured the characters from the Pixar "Inside Out" movie, we can be friends.

As I mentioned earlier, I have an addiction to anger and frustration. I will do everything possible to feel anger and frustration to get this hit, this more, this umph, because it feels good. It feels comfortable. I know it and I know it well.

As an adult, I put myself into situations where I would feel angry, because it was the most familiar feeling to me. I purposely sabotage myself by procrastinating. I'll wait until the last possible moment to leave the house and get angry at a stoplight. *A stoplight.* I'll wait until the last possible moment to begin a project which means I stay up late, which means I'm grumpy and annoyed the next day, just so I can feel frustrated.

I will find ways to pick fights with my husband or nitpick and nag and frustrate him because in my mind misery loves company. I purposefully sign up for workshops or events and then not attend thereby wasting my time AND money just so I can nibble on some Sour Cream and Angry chips.

It was at this moment, at this particular seminar (that I ACTUALLY went to), where it hit me: I had been doing all of these things because it felt comfortable to be angry. My frustration felt like a cozy blanket that I wrapped myself in on a cold winter evening.

This was the moment of truth. Would I let my addiction control me, or would I finally take control?

My addiction to anger certainly wasn't serving me. It most definitely wasn't serving my relationship (with my husband or anyone else). In fact, it was hurting me...and the people I love.

I walked out on the next break and just took a deep breath. I had to do something. I couldn't continue eating an entire bag of Sour Cream & Angry chips and pack on the weight that goes along with it.

But what to do?

Breaking the Pattern

Luckily, I realized I had already taken the first step: to SEE it by recognizing my addiction.

You can too.

It's a feeling you grew up with, you felt it consistently in your home. It was the safest emotion to feel AND express. It's also present right now in your life. It's your go-to when things aren't going your way, or when you're going after a powerful goal and things aren't working out. It's how you feel when you aren't doing what you know you should be.

It also shows up when your significant other does something that drives you nuts. How do you feel when your significant other leaves cabinet doors open? Or how about when you're getting into the car and the tank is empty? That! Right there! Whatever feeling that was, is linked to your addiction.

Now that we see it, the second step is to SAY it.

You know what your addiction is. You can identify the things that cause you to feel this feeling. Now you must tell everyone about it. I know, weird right? But stay with me.

You're going to tell your parents, your friends, your significant other... basically, anyone you interact with often.

Here's why:

When you slip—and you will, it's called being human—you'll be able to have them point it out to you. You'll also be able to call yourself out on it in front of them without them making a funny face.

For example, in the middle of a heated dialogue with my husband (because we don't argue, we dialogue), I'll stop myself and say out loud, "I'm doing it again, aren't I?" My husband will smirk, give me a kiss on the forehead, say, "I love you baby" and walk away. He knows that I know, and I don't need him to tell me.

NOW, on the other hand, if I don't recognize that I'm angry, and my addiction has taken over, I can have my people ask, "Why you angry?" That repetition helps to catch it quicker and then do something about it.

You can decide if you want to keep eating the chips or fold up the bag, put a clip on it, and shove it in the back of a very high shelf.

The last step: FORGIVE it, and yourself.

Once you find out what emotion you're addicted to, it's very easy to beat yourself up. There is a tendency to "should" on yourself and make yourself wrong. It usually sounds like, "I should have (done something different, said something different, behaved differently)."

Except, here's the thing: Little Destiny that created this addiction didn't know any better. Little Destiny did the best with what she had, and so did you.

Little Destiny had no clue that the moment this addiction was created would lead to this, and it would cause all this turmoil in life. Little Destiny didn't know any better, neither did little you. Neither does the adult sitting in your seat right now, reading this book.

This is new information, and it's easy to look back at all the events that took place and nitpick at them, and to stare at them hard, willing them to change. But they won't, and they shouldn't, because all of those moments got you here.

All those moments pushed you further than you thought you could go. All those moments pushed you outside of your comfort zone and pushed you to move and get off your behind. All of these moments put together are a part of you, and you're pretty badass.

So, forgive the past that created this trauma, and forgive yourself for unknowingly continuing it on.

Right now is the time to make this choice, to make the decision that you want something different, nay, you DESERVE something different, and you want it now.

You want to break the pattern and end this emotional addiction and choose something different, something that will serve you. Something that feels good and free, and powerful for YOU.

Now, I caution that what feels good for you may not be what feels good for someone else, so no comparing!

To have this, remember to implement these 3 steps in your life:

1. SEE it - Recognize your emotional addiction to your trauma.
2. SAY it - Tell everyone about it.
3. FORGIVE it - Forgive yourself and your trauma.

START WITH STEP ONE: what do you think *your* emotional addiction might be?

One thing is for sure: I'm not the only one out there whose addiction is anger. We're in a time where that addiction has torn us apart.

But when we see it, say it, and forgive it, we can use our anger to bring us closer together. Imagine that!

Remember:

"Anger is the only emotion that fights injustice. If your anger isn't helping you to do this, then it's not serving you at all." ~ Destiny DeHaven

DESTINY DEHAVEN

Destiny calls herself a "Pattern Breaker and Bullshit Detector." Using proven tools like Neurolinguistic Programming, the Subconscious Release Technique, and Hypnotherapy, Destiny helps stressed out, overwhelmed entrepreneurs live their most fulfilling life. Through her 4-week energy clearing sessions they stop playing small, gain clarity, and grow their business THEIR way.

Destiny loves Schitt's Creek, Spaceballs the movie, dry British wit, painting rocks, and empowering others to step into their power. She has appeared as a guest on several podcasts as well as on stage (both live and virtual). Destiny enjoys speaking about Breaking the Pattern of Procrastination, Breaking Limiting Beliefs, and Empowering Kids to be Resilient.

After moving from Hawaii to Wyoming and making a 6 year pit stop in Colorado, Destiny and her husband as well as their dog, Chance, now call Texas home.

linktr.ee/yourmagicaldestiny

RED THREAD PUBLISHING

Red Thread Publishing is an all-female publishing company on a mission to support 10,000 women to become successful published authors and thought leaders. Through the transformative work of writing & telling our stories we are not only changed as individuals, but we are also changing the global narrative & thus the world.

www.redthreadbooks.com

Publisher's Note: In order to honor and respect the voices and authenticity of each of the women who contributed to this book, we have chosen to leave the spellings of certain words to represent the country of origin of the author. For this reason you will occasionally see British spellings and alternate spellings of words. This is conscious and intentional.

THANK YOU!

Thank you so much for engaging with these stories. If you experienced any benefit, please consider doing any of the following:

• Leave a Review on **Amazon** or **Goodreads**. Your reviews help prospective readers decide if this is right for them & it is the greatest kindness you can offer the authors.

• Recommend this book to a friend.

• Join the Red Thread writers' community facebook.com/groups/redthreadwriters

• Share your own story in a collaborative author book, or a solo project.

• Live free, live fully, live your Spark!

CALL FOR SUBMISSIONS

Red Thread Publishing is calling for submissions to our **First-time Female Author Anthology: Brave New Voices.**
- Write a chapter or a short story,
- Send it to our submission committee

If selected we will publish your work in our anthology & offer you a **full scholarship** to our writer's coaching, publishing services & thought-leaders/author-preneur training.

Learn more & Send submissions: bit.ly/3mImp59

**If you don't qualify for this project & still want to write & be published, check out Red Thread's Collaborative Author projects & publishing services: https://redthreadbooks.mykajabi.com/services

We are an on-purpose, for-profit company. It costs money to produce a great book, but we acknowledge that not every voice is bankrolled. We believe every story matters, not just the stories of the women who can afford to publish them. Therefore we have built into our business structure scholarship funds using profits to support organizations for good in the world as well as our first-time authors' anthology publishing.

Website: redthreadbooks.com/

See a list of all books we

have published: redthreadbooks.mykajabi.com/books

✓ All royalties from this book are donated to the Red Thread Publishing's First-Time Female Author fund, to accomplish the mission of supporting 10,000 women to become successful published authors, entrepreneurs & thought leaders! With the purchase of this book, you are making that dream a reality for one more woman & changing the world. Thank you.

ACKNOWLEDGEMENTS

At Red Thread Publishing we often say, "If we have done our job well, no one will notice." We mean that the job of a publisher to to let the voice & content shine. So many incredible women have supported the birth of this book, and it is not enough to have their efforts be silent & invisible. In addition to the incredible contribution of each author, there are a few people who deserve to be thanked here. Mimi Rich, our faithful developmental editor, beta-reader, new author cheerleader & book grandma, thank you for always being up for anything, for your eagle eye, and your heart. Adrienne MacIain, our meticulous editor, your effort makes each of our voices ring true. Vanessa Goez, your tireless effort on the interior design of this book pulls all the other efforts together & makes our message a real book. And to each member of the Red Thread Publishing team, all your efforts, energetic & logistic, not only are bringing forth a book into the world, but now it is a world with a few more brave, bold women who are now published authors! Brava!

ALSO BY RED THREAD BOOKS

The Anatomy of a Book

Available on Amazon & everywhere books are sold.

This book brings together the tools & wisdom from publishers, book marketers, professional podcasters & public speaking coaches to teach you how to make the most of launching & selling your books, skills & services. An invaluable guide and addition to your author library.

Get your copy: redthreadbooks.mykajabi.com/anatomyofabook

See a list of all books we have published: redthreadbooks.mykajabi.com/books

FEISTY: DANGEROUSLY AMAZING WOMEN USING THEIR VOICES & MAKING AN IMPACT

How to Shine Without Shame in a World That Wants to Silence You

If you're ready to rewrite all the rules and start thriving, just as you are, then Feisty is a must-read!

WARNING: This book is not for everybody. Well-behaved women rarely make history, so, check your good-girl card at the door. There is something even better waiting on the other side if you dare venture.

Stories to inspire you to new heights of bravery, new depths of vulnerability, and new dimensions of femininity.

What does it mean to be feisty?

This collection of true tales of resistance and persistence in the face of historical oppression from cycle-breaking writers of all walks of life will defy your expectations, validate your experiences, and rally your inner warrior-woman.

Not only that, but this book also teaches you how to:

- *Identify and share your own feisty flickers and acts of brave badassery*
- *Release the "shoulds" and embrace your true desires*

- *Heal from shame and trauma*
- *Accept and embrace your authentic self*
- *Find hope and resilience in any situation*

The moment we stop judging our wishes is the moment we become capable of fulfilling them.

Order your copy of Feisty NOW!

amazon.com/gp/product/B09Q5923Y6/

See a list of all books we have published: redthreadbooks.mykajabi.com/books

SANCTUARY: CULTIVATING SAFE SPACE, REDISCOVERING THE POWER THAT UNITED US

Order your copy of SANCTUARY NOW!

A collection of stories from women who are claiming a new relationship with womanhood, with themselves & one another. Plus an invaluable tool to cultivate safe space for yourself & with women in your orbit to spread sisterhood near you.

Order Now: amazon.com/author/sierramelcher

See a list of all books we have published: redthreadbooks.mykajabi.com/books

NOTES

Unleashing Women in Leadership

1. https://www.weforum.org/reports/global-gender-gap-report-2021
2. Michael Zinnie, "In Barrier-Breaking Speech, Kamala Harris Says She May Be the First, 'But I Will Not Be the Last'" *(TIME, November 7, 2020).*
3. Kingsley Ighobor, "Celebratory rise in African women's political participation- women legislators inches upward", June 14, 2015
4. Access free training on leadership at: www.balmethod.com

Dr. Hynd Bouhia

1. www.balmethod.com

Adversity - Your Greatest Gift

1. Joe Dispenza, *Breaking The Habit of Being Yourself*, (Encephalon, LLC, 2013).

A Marketing Love Story: Ideas to change the game

1. The Ideas Factory - Is a Strategic Consultant Agency created in 2016 with the idea to support business leaders with the creative execution they need to support their marketing & sales efforts.

Made in the USA
Columbia, SC
09 June 2022